SHE PLAYS TO WIN

Desmond - thanks
for your support!
- Prabhleen

SHE PLAYS TO WIN

Prabhleen Kaur Lamba

NEW DEGREE PRESS

SHE PLAYS TO WIN

ISBN

978-1-63730-428-0   *Paperback*

978-1-63730-513-3   *Kindle Ebook*

978-1-63730-514-0   *Digital Ebook*

To My Loving Family...

Mom, Dad, and Mantej.

Thank you for always believing in me.

CONTENTS

INTRODUCTION 11

PART 1 **ISSUES IN WOMEN'S SPORTS** **17**
CHAPTER 1 STRUGGLES BEFORE TITLE IX 19
CHAPTER 2 THIRTY-SEVEN WORDS CHANGE HISTORY 25
CHAPTER 3 GENDER PAY GAP IN SPORTS 31
CHAPTER 4 NEGLECT OF WOMEN'S SPORTS 41

PART 2 **STORIES THAT INSPIRE** **49**
CHAPTER 5 ALANA NICHOLS 51
CHAPTER 6 BIGGER THAN THE GAME 59
CHAPTER 7 KRISTI YAMAGUCHI 65
CHAPTER 8 MELISSA STOCKWELL 73
CHAPTER 9 LINDSEY VONN 79
CHAPTER 10 KENDALL COYNE SCHOFIELD 85
CHAPTER 11 LAUREN FISHER 93
CHAPTER 12 REVOLUTIONIZING WOMEN'S SOCCER 99
CHAPTER 13 HILARY KNIGHT 107

PART 3 **PROGRESS AND THE FUTURE** **113**
CHAPTER 14 FEMALE COACHES IN PROFESSIONAL SPORTS 115
CHAPTER 15 WOMEN IN SPORTS MEDIA 121
CHAPTER 16 FAN ENGAGEMENT IN WOMEN'S SPORTS 127
CHAPTER 17 WORKING TOGETHER TO ADVANCE
WOMEN'S SPORTS 135
CHAPTER 18 KEEPING GIRLS IN THE GAME 141
CHAPTER 19 YOUNG GIRLS MAKING CHANGE 149

ACKNOWLEDGMENTS 159
APPENDIX 163

"My coach said I run like a girl, and I said if he ran a little faster he could too."

—MIA HAMM

INTRODUCTION

———

I have never been to a professional women's sporting event, even though I have attended many professional men's basketball, ice hockey, and football games.

Why is that?

It's not that I haven't been interested in women's sports. Ever since I started playing basketball in elementary school, I've known about the Women's National Basketball Association (WNBA) and spent time reading about female athletes and their journeys. However, even though the Bay Area has great men's basketball, football, baseball, soccer, and ice hockey teams, there aren't any professional women's sports teams in the Bay Area yet. I am excited for the future, though, as there have been talks about adding a WNBA and NWSL (National Women's Soccer League) team to the Bay Area's passionate fan base.

I have been fortunate to have the opportunity to play sports and learn about women's sports leagues since I was a young girl in elementary school, but many of my close friends have not. Professional female athletes inspire young women and prove that girls play sports too. However, many of my friends rarely saw these amazing leaders and role models being covered on television. Some may believe that men and women live in an equal world now in the twenty first century, but this is obviously not true. Even though women account for 40 percent of all athletes, out of all the sports media coverage, only 4 percent is dedicated to women's sports. (Zimbalist, 2019) That's not even close to 40 percent. If female sporting events were shown on television more often, it would help encourage female participation in sports by conveying the message to young girls that sports are for everyone, regardless of one's gender.

In addition, when female athletes are given the spotlight on television, unfortunately the focus is put on their bodies and faces, rather than their athletic abilities. Simone Biles, the most decorated gymnast of all time, explained to young women during a visit to New York's Lower Eastside Girls Club that "No matter how good you are in your sport, in life, in work, the number one thing people talk about is how you look. . . . You're still going to thrive. You're going to become somebody amazing and great. You are all beautiful, inside and out." (Aguirre, 2020) Simone shares her personal experience about the challenges female athletes like herself face and uses her story to inspire other young women to always believe in themselves.

The lack of media coverage in women's sports also leads to unequal pay. Since professional women's leagues are rarely showcased on television, they generate less revenue than male sports leagues because fewer tickets and merchandise are sold, and fewer people watch the games. Since they generate less profit, they aren't able to pay their athletes nearly as much as male athletes are paid. The unequal pay gap is present in many sports, including basketball. The average salary of an athlete of the National Basketball Association (NBA) is $7.7 million, while for the Women's National Basketball Association it is only $120,648. (Queen Ballers Club, 2020) Many WNBA players even have to play overseas during their off-season to make enough money. In 2018, about ninety out of the 144 athletes in the WNBA played overseas during their league's off-season. (Driver, 2019) This was certainly not easy as it took away the time they had to rest and recover for the next season. Also, being away from your friends and family for extended periods of time is challenging.

> Even though female athletes train and play just as hard as their male counterparts, the lack of media coverage and pay leads to their being disrespected. Devereaux Peters, a former WNBA player, says that she constantly hears people say, "A high school team could beat WNBA players." (Miller and Bissoy, 2019) Even female athletes who are just beginning their professional sports career have to deal with being disrespected, despite all the time they spend practicing and preparing for games. Nicole, a female athlete, who is also a scholarship tennis player, mentions, "We work so hard to not be respected and get credit for what we do. . . . It's insulting." (Media Coverage and Female Athletes - Full Documentary, 2015)

Another misconception that many people have believed for decades is that women's sports are not entertaining because female athletes are not skilled or competitive. This is clearly not true, as demonstrated by the United States Women's National Soccer Team. The women's soccer team has won four Olympic gold medals and has four World Cup titles. (Goal, 2021)

As shown, we still have a long way to go to achieve equal pay, respect, and media coverage in women's sports. I am compelled to write this book because I have been a female athlete all my life. The media doesn't make the public aware of women's sports, so the events aren't very accessible, which sends the wrong message to youth around the world today that girls don't belong in sports.

I have experienced on a personal level the harmful impact that this message can have. Many of my friends oftentimes say that they aren't "athletic" or "strong" enough to play sports and never will be. I remember a specific moment during my freshman year in high school that shows how the lack of visibility in professional women's sports creates barriers for young female athletes. During physical education, my classmates and I were playing basketball, and the rule was that the more games your team won, the less you had to run on mile day. When one of the boys in the class would drive in and score, they would get high fives and cheers from their teammates. However, when I did a crossover and scored a basket for my team, a boy on the other team commented that I was playing "aggressively."

My personal experiences as well as what I've learned about women's sports have inspired me to write a book about female athletes. I hope to explore the intersection of women and sports, address the aspects of media coverage and pay, and inspire other young girls to participate in athletics. I have also spent time learning about this very relevant issue and have even interviewed professional female athletes and women's sports advocates for this book. I want to share the inspirational journeys of female athletes to motivate girls and women to participate in sports. Female athletes deserve equal pay, respect, and media coverage—and in this book I explain why. This book is not only for girls and women, but also for anyone who wants to see this issue addressed and see change in society.

From the passage of Title IX and Billie Jean King's victory in the "Battle of the Sexes" tennis match in the early 1970s, women's sports have come a long way. (Billie Jean King, 2021) Kendall Coyne Schofield has created new opportunities by participating in the NHL All-Star Skills Competition. (Kendall Coyne, 2020) Becky Hammon, a former WNBA player, has become a trailblazer as an NBA assistant coach. (Chappell, 2020) Women, such as Alana Nichols, have also made strides in the field of adaptive sports. (Alana Nichols | 60 MINUTES SPORTS Full Segment, 2016) Every day, female athletes are breaking down barriers and opening doors. Professional athletes from men's sports leagues are also speaking up and advocating to help advance women's sports. However, there is still a long road ahead to achieve equal pay, respect, and media coverage in female athletics. My goal is to motivate people by sharing the inspirational stories of female athletes and advance the work that is being done to achieve gender equality.

PART I

ISSUES IN WOMEN'S SPORTS

STRUGGLES
BEFORE TITLE IX

———

"You have intramural sports; that should be enough." This
statement was what twin sisters Diane and Suzanne Strain,
later known as Diane McClelland and Suzanne Lackman,
told me they received in 1957 when they were high school
freshmen at David Douglas High School (DDHS) and asked
their school administrator if they could start a girls' tennis team. Since a new boys' tennis team was being created,
Suzanne responded to the school administrator, "We want to
have an interscholastic team like the boys." Diane explained
that she and her sister wanted to form a tennis team for girls
"because we have been playing tennis since we were in third
grade and love the sport. And there was no way for us to play
competitively in grade school." When I heard this, I couldn't
even imagine going through elementary school without playing competitive sports because they have always been such
an important aspect in my life; in elementary school, I did
gymnastics and played basketball. Sharing the stories of girls
who were refused the opportunity to play sports, which led

to their creating their own space in the field, is critical to illustrating how hard fought this battle has been.

Back then, young girls rarely played competitive sports, as they received far fewer opportunities than boys, faced many barriers, and were mainly restricted to participating in recreational sports. Title IX was a law passed in 1972 "to provide everyone with equal access to any program or activity that receives Federal financial assistance, including sports." (Women's Sports Foundation, 2016) However, in 1957, when Diane and Suzanne wanted to form their own girls' sports team, this law had not yet been passed. The Women's Sports Foundation reported in 2016 that before Title IX was passed, only "one in twenty-seven girls played sports."

Suzanne shared with me that she did some research and discovered that when she was trying to start a girls' tennis team at the high school she attended with Diane, the boys had more than eight competitive sports teams. Counting varsity, junior varsity, and freshmen teams, they had a total of sixteen, whereas the girls had none. Although the school administration initially refused to allow girls to have a competitive tennis team, Diane and Suzanne did not back down and made their point clear—they wanted to have an interscholastic sports team like the boys.

After giving it some thought, the administration agreed that if Diane and Suzanne could get fifty girls to turn out, they might consider the idea, even though there was only a need to select six girls for the team. The girls took on the challenge and started their campaign right away to recruit players. Suzanne reported, "Diane and I did public address announcements, created and hung posters around the school, resulting in a surprising total of sixty girls turning out for the team. The girls were very excited about the results and some of the teachers were very supportive, too." The administration, aware of the large turnout, held a two-day tryout and selected six girls to form the first girls' competitive sports team started at David Douglas High School.

When I asked Diane and Suzanne about what inspired them to persevere despite facing challenges, they mentioned they were raised in a family where "nothing stands in the way but you," as their grandfather and uncle were also professional baseball players. Suzanne explained, "With that in mind, we decided we're not going to let the high school administration decide whether we can play tennis or not." As time went on, the administration, which included the superintendent, principal, and athletic director, started supporting the girls' tennis team. They even thanked Diane and Suzanne and mentioned they were so glad the girls had started the tennis team.

The following year, in 1958, the David Douglas High School girls' tennis team won the Oregon State Championship. This became the first time any sports team at DDHS had won a state championship. Although they might not have known this at the time, Diane and Suzanne had made a lasting impact on girls' sports in their school district, which would be felt even sixty years later!

In 2017, more than half a century after starting the girls' tennis team, David Douglas High School invited Diane and Suzanne to come watch one of their girls' tennis matches. When they showed up, they "were honored with flowers and handwritten thank-you notes from the girls who now numbered twenty-two on their team." Also, when David Douglas was playing against Gresham, a longtime rival, athletes from the two high school teams got together and made an arch with their tennis rackets that they had Diane and Suzanne go through. They mentioned that the coach was truly appreciative that Diane and Suzanne had started a girls' tennis team at DDHS. The high school girls were almost in tears and amazed that Diane and Suzanne created this all-girls sports team, even though they were told they couldn't have one.

Suzanne mentioned, "That's what amazes me and that's why I like to constantly, continually, remind young people, there's been a lot of things standing in our girls' and women's way. . . . Just because someone says you can't do it, that doesn't mean it can't be done. You can rise above it and accomplish it." The principal and athletic director announced during this event that Diane and Suzanne not only started the first DDHS girls' tennis team but also inspired the league of over ten high schools to start girls' interscholastic team sports.

When I asked Diane how she felt about this experience, she explained that it "really underscored the importance that if you feel strongly about an idea that could possibly help others, to be strong and courageous and to push forward because you just never know." This idea encourages others to pursue their dreams as well. One of the most exciting parts of being a mentor, as she mentioned, is that you may not even know the people you're already touching: "It kind of creates responsibility for all of us. If we know something is important, we should increase the opportunity for our voices to be heard, because that incentivizes others to speak up and say,

'Wow, that's great that she did that. I think I would like to do that in the future.'" Suzanne also agrees with this, saying, "It's amazing how you can come up with an idea and it can end up impacting so many more lives than you ever would have dreamed."

Diane and Suzanne have continued to make a difference in the lives of many other girls outside of their school district. Together, they have founded the Girls S.T.E.A.M. Institute, a nonprofit organization whose acronym stands for science, technology, engineering, art/athletics, and math. Their "goal is to provide a framework and platform that informs, inspires and empowers young girls to explore entrepreneurial opportunities that can change the world through S.T.E.A.M." (Girls S.T.E.A.M. Institute, 2021) The sisters explained that the importance of creating opportunities for girls and women in sports is that it gives them self-confidence and also teaches teamwork and collaboration.

Diane pointed out that "You can lose, but then you can win the next time. Losing is not failure. Losing is part of our life experience, and sports is a great illustration of that: we practice, we prepare, and we play. And we play to the best of our ability. But sometimes we lose, but that's just part of the game of sports." They also emphasized that it is important for young girls to learn how to work in a team toward a common goal. Suzanne shared that from her personal experiences, women who have the best skills for running a business learned how to create a culture of teamwork since they participated in team sports.

In 2017, a local newspaper covered their journey as advocates for women's sports. When they were initially told no, Suzanne mentioned, "Being fourteen and facing that rejection, we were shocked we were told that we couldn't do it." Diane said, "We just felt that it was something important that we needed to do. We didn't think the situation was fair or equitable, but we had no idea the impact it would have over the next sixty years." (Rawlings, 2017) This newspaper also wrote about how meaningful this experience was for the sisters throughout their high school years and how it inspired Suzanne and Diane to continue the fight for equal rights for girls and women for many years to come.

Diane shared that "having that experience in high school was really the catalyst for having this focus on helping women and girls for all these years. What we do here [in their nonprofit organization] has become a pinnacle part of this extension to help women receive the equality that they need." For Suzanne, this experience not only motivated her to become an advocate for equal rights for women but also inspired her to always stand up for all those who are treated unfairly: "And I expand that to everyone who isn't empowered. We are all like links in a chain; if there is a weak link, then the whole chain is weak." (Rawlings, 2017)

In the future, Diane and Suzanne hope to see girls being encouraged to go and try out any sport they want to, being paid equitably, and being given the same support and recognition for their athletic abilities that boys are given. Diane mentioned that this "helps create that inner confidence to say, 'Wow, I can do this.'" Suzanne added, "It gives them the courage and power to try other new things that may be kind of scary at first, like starting a new business or career, but they get it done successfully."

THIRTY-SEVEN WORDS
CHANGE HISTORY

———

Title IX is often referred to as the "thirty-seven words that changed everything." (Billie Jean King, 2021)

The passage of this law in 1972, along with the "Battle of the Sexes" tennis match in 1973, changed the field of women's sports forever. However, there were many challenges involved in the path to this victory in the early 1970s. Much of the credit for this historic moment in sports is given to Billie Jean King, who worked tirelessly then and still does to this day, to advance equality. (Billie Jean King, 2021)

Growing up, Billie Jean was surrounded by athletic family members and played many sports, including basketball, softball, and tennis. She started playing tennis in fifth grade, and after playing the sport for the first time at a country club, she knew it was the one she wanted to pursue for the rest of her life. She told her mom, "I am going to be number one in the world." (Billie Jean King, 2021)

King quickly came to know about the discrimination young female athletes faced through her own personal experience. In 1955, she participated in a tennis competition at a club in Los Angeles. When the players gathered to take a picture, Billie Jean was excluded from it because instead of wearing a dress, she was wearing shorts that her mom had sewn for her. She made a promise to herself when she was only twelve years old: "I want to make a difference in the lives of others." (Billie Jean King, 2021)

Despite early challenges, like the one she faced in 1955, King stayed dedicated to the sport. After becoming a professional athlete in 1958, she quickly made her name well known around the world. She and her teammate became the youngest pair to win the women's Wimbledon doubles championship in 1961. After this, Billie Jean's accolades started piling up. She won the singles Wimbledon championship for three years in a row, along with the US and Australian Open singles titles. Altogether, she won thirty-nine Grand Slam titles during her professional tennis career. King's childhood dream came true in 1966, when she became the number one female tennis player in the world. She was also ranked number one in the world several other times and held the honorable ranking for a total of six years. (Billie Jean King, 2021)

Although King had achieved everything in the sport of tennis that people imagined was possible, her most historic win was yet to come. During the seventies, she was a powerful fighter in the women's rights movement. Using her platform, she fought for equality and leveraged her voice to provide equal opportunities for all. (Billie Jean King, 2021)

One of the problems she worked to address was the gender pay gap in sports. Although she had become the first female athlete to be awarded over $100,000 as a prize for winning a match, she received $15,000 less than the winner of the men's tournament in the 1972 US Open. This pushed King to campaign for men and women tennis players to be awarded equal prize money; she became a part of the "Original 9", a group of female tennis players that protested against unequal prize money. The US Open eventually did make the prize money equal for both genders' competitions and all the Grand Slams Tournaments that followed too. Billie Jean also formed the Women's Tennis Association in 1973 to help female tennis players get the acknowledgment they deserve. (Billie Jean King, 2021)

Around the same time period, she was working to help pass Title IX. At the time, only 1 percent of college money budgeted to athletics went to female sports, and the ratio of male to female high school athletes was twelve to five. King testified in Washington, DC, where she gave a speech about the importance of Title IX in helping female athletes progress in sports. On June 23, 1972, Title IX was passed, and the thirty-seven words written in the law made a lasting impact on women's athletics, ensuring that nobody would "be subjected to discrimination under any education program or activity receiving Federal financial assistance." (NCAA, 2021) That same year, Billie Jean King became the first woman to be chosen as *Sports Illustrated*'s Sportsperson of the Year. (Billie Jean King, 2021)

Although there is still a lot of work to do in advancing female sports, Title IX has helped high school girls' participation in sports increase by 1,057 percent and college girls' increase by 614 percent. (Billie Jean King, 2021) More women are also pursuing sports as a professional career. King explains that "the passage of Title IX legislation in 1972 opened important doors, but I knew it would take long-term and continued efforts and dedication to ensure those doors remained open." (King, 2011)

Shortly after the passage of Title IX, Billie Jean King would compete in the most-watched tennis match in history. Bobby Riggs, who was once number one in the world for men's tennis and fifty-five years old at the time, disparaged women's sports and claimed that even someone as old as him could defeat the women's top tennis players. Although King had refused to play in other challenges Riggs had offered before, she accepted the one in 1973. The match, King versus Riggs, became known as the "Battle of the Sexes" and was viewed by about ninety million people across the globe. It took place in Houston on September 20, 1973. (Billie Jean King, 2021)

King recognized that she had to come home with the victory because Title IX was just passed the previous year, and she wanted to use the "Battle of the Sexes" tournament to help people's mindsets parallel what was written in the legislation. But, with King, there was always a duality to everything she did, and this was no different. She explained that:

"I wanted to beat Bobby Riggs because it was one year after Title IX was passed. I wanted to change the hearts and minds of people. And as we know, to change hearts and minds to match the law isn't that easy. So I had to beat him for a lot of reasons. But it wasn't about a tennis match—it was about social change." (Burk, 2012)

Billie Jean King successfully defeated Bobby Riggs in the "Battle of the Sexes" tennis match and even won in three consecutive sets, six to four, six to four, and six to three. This victory was a historic moment and paved the way for female athletes to continue advancing in sports. King ended up writing a book about this experience, which she published in 2008, and a movie was made about it and released in 2017. (Billie Jean King, 2021)

She also recalls that the timing of this event made it an iconic moment in history, since women's rights were really heating up in 1973. Billie Jean made a lasting impact on women's sports that night and fulfilled the promise she made when she was twelve years old. Looking back on the moment, the "Battle of the Sexes" also demonstrated the gender inequality in sports media coverage as the sportscaster focused the coverage on King's looks rather than on her accomplishments. (Chapin, 2017)

Even after winning this notable tennis match, Billie Jean continued her work to make a difference in the lives of others. She co-founded an organization in which men and women play tennis together. World TeamTennis, which started in 1974, is one of the proudest parts of her life because in this league, men and women compete together on equal terms. (Billie Jean King, 2021)

During the same year, King also founded the Women's Sports Foundation, an organization that protects Title IX, funds research about equity, and advocates in support of female athletes. She started another initiative in 2014, called the Billie Jean King Leadership Initiative (BJKLI), which is dedicated to promoting equality and inclusion and advocating for equal pay for equal work. (BJKLI, 2021)

Billie Jean has been inducted into several halls of fame and has been recognized with some of the most honorable awards. She was named one of the "100 Most Important Americans of the 20th Century" by *LIFE* Magazine in 1990 and one of the Greatest Athletes of the Century by *Sports Illustrated* in 1999. On August 12, 2009, she was awarded the Presidential Medal of Freedom at the White House by former President Barack Obama. (Billie Jean King, 2021) During the ceremony, President Obama mentioned, "We honor what she [Billie Jean King] calls 'all of the off the court stuff.' What she did to broaden the reach of the game, to change how women athletes and women everywhere view themselves, and to give everyone, regardless of gender or sexual orientation, including my two daughters, a chance to compete both on the court and in life." (Presidential Medal of Freedom 2009 Ceremony - Presented by President Barack Obama, 2011)

A trailblazer and leader in women's sports, Billie Jean King has been instrumental in advancing women's athletics. She continues working on many initiatives to this day and says that women don't need to be happy just accepting the crumbs, but "have the cake, the icing and the cherry on top too." (Barajas, 2016)

GENDER PAY GAP
IN SPORTS

———

In fifth and sixth grade, during my last two years in elementary school, my friends and I played together on the school
basketball team and won two consecutive championships.
Our lives revolved around basketball—we played it, talked
about it, and also watched professional athletes play it on
TV. We all had this dream that when we grew up, we would
be basketball players. However, one day we discovered that
WNBA (Women's National Basketball Association) players are
not even paid close to how much NBA (National Basketball
Association) players are paid. All these years, we had been
watching both the men's and women's leagues play and never
thought that such a wide gender pay gap in sports could
possibly even exist.

We also found out that during the off season, when athletes are
supposed to be resting and spending time with their families,
many WNBA players were actually playing abroad so that
they could earn enough money. After this realization, many

of my friends and I started questioning ourselves and thought, "Maybe we don't want to be professional basketball players after all." This sparked my interest in doing more research about the gender pay gap in sports and showed to me how big of a problem this is—something I didn't know when I was in elementary school. The most surprising statistic I found was that only two out of the top one hundred highest-paid athletes are women. (Price, 2020)

I shared this personal story in a conversation with Dr. Ellen J. Staurowsky, a sports media professor in the Roy H. Park School of Communications at Ithaca College. She is "internationally recognized as an expert on social justice issues in sport which include gender equity and Title IX, pay equity and equal employment opportunity, [and] . . . representation of women in sport media." Dr. Staurowsky is the author and editor of a book, *Women and Sport: Continuing a Journey of Liberation and Celebration*, and "as a researcher and advocate on behalf of women in sport," she has been a lead and co-author of many reports about girls' and women's sports. She has received many honors for her work in this field, including the Women's Sports Foundation Researcher of the Year award and the National Association for Girls and Women in Sports President's Award. (Ithaca College, 2021) When Dr. Staurowsky asked how the issue of gender pay gap in sports came to my attention, I told her about my experiences in elementary school.

She responded, "What you just said really is what drives me to work on these issues and to take them on and to educate people; and to challenge them in terms of decision-makers and what they're doing, because you know your comment that in discovering that [the gender pay gap in sports], it becomes discouraging to think about pursuing a career in sports is exactly the reason why this has to be fixed. You know, no girl going through the sport system should ever have to consider her future on the basis of seeing that females are not being treated fairly because that just perpetuates this injustice."

When I asked Dr. Staurowsky about the roots and historical background of the gender pay gap in sports, she explained that in this country, forever, we've had a situation in which women's work has been undervalued. One of the turning points was during the Victorian Era, when people were moving from farms to cities, causing the social arrangement to change. This resulted in the idea, which coincided with one from the first industrial revolutions, that men were going to work in factories while women stayed at home. Men would be in the public sphere, while women were in the private sphere. From this, an economic argument emerged that men were going to be the breadwinners and women would take care of the family.

Dr. Staurowsky mentioned, "Conceptually, the work that women were assigned to do became thought of as being less important." Although the history of this goes back a long way, it continues to play out in all kinds of professions in our world today and also serves as the foundation of the gender pay gap in sports. This leads to many of our modern-day problems, including women's sports not being taken seriously, female athletes being dismissed, women coaches not being viewed as equal partners, and administrations not promoting women's sports the way that they should be. Through my research and interview with Dr. Staurowsky, I explored the issues faced by female athletes in three sports—ice hockey, basketball, and soccer.

In March of 2017, the United States Women's National Ice Hockey Team planned a boycott and announced that they would not participate in the International Ice Hockey Federation world championship "after negotiations for an increase in wages and support from USA Hockey stalled." Meghan Duggan, who was then the captain of the team, stated, "We are asking for a living wage and for USA Hockey to fully support its programs for women and girls and stop treating us like an afterthought. We have represented our country with dignity and deserve to be treated with fairness and respect." (Berkman, 2017)

To get a deeper look into this issue, I interviewed Meghan about her experience in leading her team in this fight for equal pay and treatment. She shared that along with winning a gold medal at the 2018 Winter Olympics in Korea with her teammates, the fight for gender equality in ice hockey is among her most memorable experiences: "Everything we learned through that process, how we pushed our sport forward; it changed all of us, the way that we see the game, see the world, and want to be able to use our platforms to continue to advocate." For one year, the team worked with lawyers and USA Hockey behind closed doors. After not being able to make significant progress, the story went public and the athletes were able to leverage the power of the media to spread their message. Their ask was centered around three main areas: support (travels, meals, hotel accommodations, insurance), marketing (promoting the women's game like the men's so more girls are encouraged to play), and increased programming (opportunity to play more games).

When I asked Duggan what gave her and her team the courage and perseverance needed to advocate for something they felt strongly about, she responded: "I think all of us, sticking together, being united, having that one voice, [and] supporting each other. It went on for probably eighteen months or so from start to finish. Being able to kind of lean on each other in those times of need and communicate and support each other through all the different ups and downs we had throughout the process was really where we continue to draw strength and, you know, the courage that you talked about to do something like that." Their mission was not only that they were fighting for their own team, but also for young girls and women in all sports. Much like in our everyday lives, when we are united with our friends and family, we have the courage and support to do what we feel is correct, just like these women.

The women's ice hockey team did end up making a deal with USA Hockey and competed in the International Ice Hockey Federation world championship. The deal included "the formation of a Women's High Performance Advisory Group to advance women's and girls' hockey at youth levels," increased salary, and the same travel services that the men's team gets. (Berkman, 2017) Meghan shared that this was a huge success, and it was so meaningful because her team continued to speak out and advocate for all girls and women.

However, this did not resolve all the issues, because in 2019, it was reported that "USA Hockey declined repeated requests to discuss the group" that was formed two years ago. Angela Ruggiero, a highly accomplished ice hockey player, commented, "There are great people at the top that care about women's hockey, but you absolutely don't have the numbers to have a real change. We have an extremely long way to go." (Berkman, 2019)

Meghan Duggan recently retired in 2020 but is continuing her advocacy work by serving on the Board of Trustees for the Women's Sports Foundation and being a part of the NHL (National Hockey League) Player Inclusion Committee. She hopes to continue to have an impact on sports and advocate for underrepresented groups in sports. At the roots of what's most important to her is ensuring that women and young girls stay in sports: "I hope that someday we get to a place where girls and women are respected, supported, and compensated in the same way that men are in professional sports, whether that be the athletes on the field, the coaches, or the front office staff in both female and male professional leagues." She explained that this is a crucial time to work toward those goals, and to get there, it takes a lot of hardworking people on both sides—women and men.

In professional basketball, the pay gap between WNBA and NBA players is not even close. The huge difference in male and female basketball players' salaries was also the statistic that drove my friends and me away from our dream of pursuing basketball as a career. NBC News reported in 2020 that while the average salary for an NBA player during the 2020 season was $7.5 million, it was only $116,000 for WNBA players. Recently, the WNBA agreed on a collective bargaining agreement, which allows top players to be paid more than three times their current salaries. (Delmore, 2020) Dr. Staurowsky explained that a raise in salary wasn't the only thing that came out of this agreement. Other issues were also addressed, including workplace protections, travel demands, and accommodations, such as the hotels WNBA players were staying in while playing in the bubble during COVID-19, which is an enclosed area they stayed in during the 2020 season. All these concerns are significant because they impact the quality of performance that WNBA athletes are able to produce.

Nneka Ogwumike, president of the WNBA Players Association, echoed this idea in a news interview with NBC News: "I think we realized that it was more than just equal pay. It was equality and fighting for what we deserve moving forward." Sue Bird, a WNBA star who has been an active advocate for female athletes, mentioned, "It's uncomfortable to have to walk into a room and speak of your own value and tell people you're valuable, [but] it's incredibly important because you can't wait for somebody else to advocate for you." (Delmore, 2020)

Another women's sports league that has been fighting to close the gender pay gap in sports is the United States Women's National Soccer Team (USWNT). Dr. Staurowsky shared with me that the team was able to argue using federal laws that protected their rights, including Title VII and the Equal Pay Act. ESPN staff reported that on March 8, 2019, the USWNT filed a gender-discrimination lawsuit against the US Soccer Federation. Even though the women's team has won four World Cup titles, documents obtained by *The Guardian* show that "the current labor agreements with US Soccer would pay each member of the women's team about $260,000 for winning a World Cup, compared with more than $1.1 million for each men's player." The women's soccer team quickly drew a lot of support from politicians and celebrities for their push to advocate for change. Fans also started chanting "Equal pay!" during the World Cup games. (Pound, 2019) ESPN staff reported that during the lawsuit, Carlos Cordeiro, the president of the United States Soccer Federation at the time, tried showing that the female soccer players were paid less because they did not perform of equal skill compared to their male counterparts. He later resigned because of strong disapproval from fans and sponsors of the US Women's National Team. (ESPN staff, 2020)

On May 1, the team encountered another setback when the court dismissed their case because they claimed that the women's team had in fact been "paid more on both a cumulative and an average per-game basis." Megan Rapinoe, a soccer star and leader in the fight for equal pay, commented on the court's decision and reasoning: "If I earn one dollar every time I play and a man earns three dollars, just because I win ten games and he only wins three games—and so I make ten dollars and he made nine dollars—I'm not sure how that's me making more money." (Reuters, 2020) Dr. Staurowsky shared that the athletes eventually did agree to a contract under duress, meaning that it was the best contract they could get. They made it clear to everybody that it was not something they were actually agreeing to, but they signed the contract because their season would have been in jeopardy; they had to reach closure so that they could continue playing and at least get paid. This was also an example of a situation that women have been navigating for many decades: having to challenge the inequality they are facing without losing their job or getting in trouble for it. Despite encountering many obstacles, the USWNT and its dedicated players are continuing to advocate for the equal pay they deserve.

By hearing the perspectives of athletes, advocates, and researchers, I have come to realize how big the gender pay gap in sports is and how every day, it is sending the wrong message to young girls in sports that they are not considered equal to boys. However, as Dr. Staurowsky mentioned, we do have the power to make this situation better, and the momentum is heading us in the right direction of change happening sooner rather than later. The inequities women face in sports are similar to those faced by women in the workplace. Therefore, female athletes and sports teams are essentially fighting for all women.

NEGLECT OF
WOMEN'S SPORTS

———

Every year, our basketball coach would assign us "homework" during the months of March and April. Our assignment was to watch the National Collegiate Athletic Association (NCAA) March Madness games on television. This is a tournament in which college basketball teams compete to win the championship, and there is a competition held for both men's and women's teams. I always worked on improving my skills by learning from the college athletes' style of play. Although I had followed the games for both the men's and women's teams every year, in 2019 I realized that not everyone valued the women's college basketball tournament. After reading about how prevalent the neglect of women's sports was in the 2019 March Madness Tournament and seeing it play out in social media and news outlets, the way I viewed gender equality in sports changed forever.

In this college tournament, female basketball players were specifically ignored and undervalued by magazines and the

NCAA itself. During the tournament, the lack of stories dedicated to the women's games in the sports section of the *USA Today* magazine demonstrated a clear neglect of women's sports. Andrew Zimbalist shared on *Forbes* that the March Madness games occurred from March 22 to April 2, and during that time period:

- Ten of the ninety-two stories written in the magazine were about women (11 percent).

- Four of the eighty-nine pictures of the athletes were of women (4 percent).

- One of the thirty-eight front page magazine pictures was of a woman (3 percent).

- One of the thirty-two athlete front page stories was about a female athlete (3 percent).

None of these percentages are even close to half.

This underrepresentation of women in sports disrespected all those female college basketball teams who had worked so hard to qualify for the tournament. Also, it wrongly showed to every young girl who had read that magazine that women don't belong in sports.

Even though women's college basketball has been growing over the years, it is still ignored by the NCAA itself. More and more people watch the NCAA Women's Final Four every year, and in 2019, the NCAA Women's Basketball Championship had its highest attendance in fifteen years. (Durham, 2019)

Despite this, the NCAA has still treated the women's teams as having little to no value. The NCAA awards the men's teams' conferences more than $1.6 million per win. The women's teams' conferences are given zero dollars per win. (Zimbalist, 2019) That's right, absolutely nothing.

While I believe the NCAA should work to promote both its men's and women's tournaments, it actually did quite the opposite. Not only did I learn the female athletes weren't rewarded for their wins like the male athletes were, but I also found that the NCAA completely disregarded the women's games in 2019.

On March 25, the NCAA made a post on Twitter that said, "When you find out there are no #MarchMadness games until Thursday." Beneath this message, there was a short clip of an actor from a TV show throwing his computer in the trash can because he was upset that no March Madness games were going on. However, there were actually eight March Madness women's games on March 25, 2019. (Negley, 2019) This tweet drew a lot of backlash from basketball fans—it was outrageous that the NCAA didn't consider their own women's tournament as a part of March Madness. Many fans tweeted that there were actually some great women's games going on that day and the tweet was totally disrespectful to all the hardworking female athletes. Breanna Stewart, a four-time NCAA Champion and three-time WNBA Champion, responded, "Sounds about right, coming from a page that has posted nothing about the women's tournament. How can we get others to respect us when the NCAA doesn't?!" (Negley, 2019)

Some people brought up the fact that the NCAA March Madness page mentioned in its bio that it was dedicated to men's basketball and that women's basketball was being talked about on a separate Twitter page. However, this also made the NCAA look bad, because it showed it didn't include the women's tournament as a part of March Madness. Stewart once again spoke out and explained that March Madness is considered to be gender neutral. (Negley, 2019) Rather than encouraging fans to watch the female athletes compete in their March Madness Tournament, the NCAA completely disregarded its games.

This tweet led to the topic of women's sports being inferior to men's sports, which sparked another discussion. I, along with others, wondered, If "March Madness" only referred to men's basketball, then did that mean we had to specifically say "Women's March Madness" if we were talking about the female athletes' tournament? Otherwise, why is the default always referencing men's sports? Shouldn't it be "Men's March Madness" and "Women's March Madness" if men and women are truly equal in the sports world?

Although I had been watching the NCAA March Madness Tournaments every year, in 2019 I realized that women's sports were still being neglected in today's society and that we had to continue the fight for gender equality in sports.

Most recently, in the 2021 NCAA Women's Basketball Tournament, gender inequities were evident once again. There were many differences between the men's and women's tournaments, including the men's teams having a full buffet while the women's teams were given prepackaged meals. Also, the men's teams were provided a full weight room with workout equipment, while the women's teams "weight room" consisted of a few mats and a small rack of dumbbells that only went up to thirty pounds. The NCAA did eventually build a new weight room for the women's teams after many players, coaches, and fans called the organization out on social media for their lack of equality. (Azzi, 2021)

I spoke to Professor Marie Hardin, the Dean of the Donald P. Bellisario College of Communications at Penn State University, about this issue. She has expertise in women in media, sports journalism, and Title IX. (PennState Donald P. Bellisario College of Communications, 2021) When I asked her why female athletes are given such less media attention and who is responsible for this, she mentioned, "A lot of this goes back to gender roles and norms that have been in place for many, many decades here in the US. . . . It's really a very deep-seated problem. There's no one single entity that should take the blame." Rather, she explained that it is a shared responsibility in terms of production and consumption. It's a shared practice between the media outlets who make the decision not to cover men's and women's sports equally and a public that has been unwilling to demand, en masse, changes in coverage of women's sports.

Oftentimes, Professor Hardin hears people say that they think more women's sports should be covered. However, when she asks them if they would watch it, they hesitate a bit. Therefore, "What we need are people who will demand coverage but then will also consume, because it's one thing to demand, but if you're not consuming, you're not helping solve the problem." We must collectively make an argument to media outlets on the basis of ethical grounds about making a contribution to a more fair and equitable society.

We have to encourage them to do the right thing—provide coverage of women's sports.

One possible solution to the problem of unequal media coverage in women's sports that I discussed with Professor Hardin was having more female sports journalists. She mentioned that simply having more women in the media would help tremendously because it would lead to diversity of perspective at the table and widen the discussion. This would ultimately make a difference in equalizing media coverage in sports.

Through my personal experience as a female athlete, combined with the research I did and the discussion I had with Professor Marie Hardin, I have learned that there is still work to be done in advocating for equal media coverage in women's sports.

PART II

STORIES THAT INSPIRE

ALANA NICHOLS

—

Alana Nichols has made history by becoming the first female American to win a gold medal in both the summer and winter Olympic Games. This is already a remarkable accomplishment on its own, but what makes her story even more inspiring is the fact that she won these gold medals in two of the hardest adaptive sports: wheelchair basketball and alpine skiing.

Alana shared with me that at the age of five, she was adopted by her grandparents. Her grandma first put her in T-ball and noticed that she had a fair amount of athletic ability, even for a five-year-old. Soon, she started playing basketball and volleyball, always staying motivated by her grandma, who was in the front row at all of Alana's games.

In high school, she pursued volleyball and softball, while also developing an interest in snowboarding. Being from northern New Mexico, she lived a few minutes away from a ski resort, which led to her becoming an all-around athlete and developing a passion for snowboarding.

"My senior year of high school, it was November 19, 2000. I was really hoping to go to college on a softball scholarship. I actually was out snowboarding and I attempted a back flip on my snowboard. I over rotated the back flip and landed on a rock that was under the snow and became paralyzed after breaking my back in three places."

Alana was seventeen years old at the time and had been an athlete all her life. She thought her athletic career was over, but it was actually just about to begin. However, at that time, Alana was not aware of what her future held. In the "Alana Nichols: 60 Minutes Sports" documentary, she referred to this time in her life as the "dark period": "I didn't want to be seen in a wheelchair. I didn't want to go out in public. I didn't want to talk to people. I didn't want to be who I was anymore. It didn't make sense to me how an athlete who very much enjoyed, celebrated her body and was able to use it every day, would then be put into a cage and confined to a wheelchair."

During this time, Alana thought that her dream of going to college on an athletic scholarship had been crushed. I can only imagine how she overcame such a difficult challenge so early on in her life.

"Eventually, it was about two years after my injury when I had to kind of recognize the fact that I was paralyzed. And I probably would be for the rest of my life. And it was when I had that realization that I needed to do the best I could with what I had, instead of comparing myself, that I really kind of blossomed into an athlete."

Two years into Alana's undergraduate career at the University of New Mexico, she discovered adaptive sports, which are sports with modifications so athletes with disabilities can also participate. (Presagia Sports, 2018) She was rolling through a gym and saw a whole team of athletes playing wheelchair basketball. Since she hadn't really seen adaptive sports before and didn't know anything about the Paralympics at that time; this was a jaw dropping moment for her. According to the International Paralympic Committee, the Paralympics, which run at the same time as the Olympics, currently consist of twenty-eight sports.

"That same day, I got into a basketball chair. I immediately felt more athletic. And I essentially ran for the first time in two years since an accident. Most importantly, I met other people with disabilities that were doing the best that they could with the bodies that they hav,e and I was really kind of left without a choice."

Alana knew that she could play sports like the people she met that day and wanted to prove this to herself. Although it was undoubtedly a tough time for her, she was inspired after meeting other athletes with disabilities who participated in adaptive sports. I know from personal experience as well that wheelchair basketball is not an easy sport. In middle school, my teammates and I participated in a fundraiser in which we played a game against the Golden State Road Warriors, an official team of the NWBA (National Wheelchair Basketball Association). It was not only difficult to shoot a basketball while sitting, but we also had to push our wheelchair while simultaneously dribbling the ball.

A year later, Alana learned about the Paralympics and the possibility of her playing on the United States Women's

Basketball Team. She decided to transfer to the University of Arizona to play on their all-women's wheelchair basketball team and pursue her ultimate dream of going to college on an athletic scholarship. She went face first into the adaptive sports world and never looked back; it was a risk, but Alana was willing to do the work to play at the varsity college level.

She trained with the Paralympic team for five years, developing her skills and personal character. A lot of responsibility comes with representing the United States on a national level, and there is a lot of hard work and training involved physically too. This experience transformed Alana from a place of a young teenager in college to a responsible adult. Even though she was pressured to perform, Alana viewed this pressure as a privilege, because it made her grow in ways that she wouldn't have otherwise. She faced many challenges to perform well under difficult circumstances, and she did.

"I think, in the end, when you are under pressure, and you're challenged, and you rise to the occasion, you really prove to yourself how strong you are and what you're made of, and I couldn't deny that."

All the hard work and determination definitely paid off, because Alana won the Olympic gold medal at the 2008 Beijing Games as a part of the US Women's Paralympic Basketball Team. (Showtime Sports, 2016)

Later on, Alana moved up to a small town in Colorado called Winter Park that has a competitive program called the National Sports Center for the Disabled. Here, Alana was reintroduced to the snow and became determined to get back on it. Although she could not ski independently at first, she quickly equipped herself with the skills she needed to compete on an international level by learning and developing the foundations of a ski racer.

Alana shared with me that in 2010, she was able to go to the Paralympics as a rookie and was on the developmental team for alpine skiing. She was willing to go back on the snow, and she won two golds, a silver, and a bronze at the 2010 Vancouver Games. Alana made history during these Olympic Games by becoming the first female American to win gold at both the summer and winter games.

Alana also competed in the 2012 London Games, where she placed fourth as a part of the US Women's Wheelchair Basketball Team. She even returned to the snow at the 2014 Sochi Games, winning another Olympic silver medal in alpine skiing. (SHOWTIME Sports, 2016)

Nichols' incredible sports journey did not end there. She mentioned in our conversation that she learned how to surf and fell in love with the water, which introduced her to paddling. By learning sprint kayaking, she became a triple-sport athlete. Although Alana did not have the time she needed to prepare herself to win a medal in this difficult sport, she qualified for the 2016 Rio Games within two years. She finished seventh at the games, making her a five-time Paralympian.

"I finished seventh. But that experience was really important for me because it was more about the process. I knew I wasn't going to win; it was more about proving to myself how hard I could work and what I was made of. The sport required me to wake up at 4:30 a.m. every morning, get on the water at six, and paddle for hours on."

Even after competing in the Paralympics five times, Alana stays involved in several sports. She also works to advance adaptive surfing and hopefully make it a Paralympic sport in 2028. Alana is a leader and motivational speaker who uses her platform to give back to the community.

"I think every athlete comes to that point in their career when they retire from performing and then you're just moved to give back because of how much it gave you."

She served as president of the Women's Sports Foundation in 2020, whose main mission is to create opportunities for girls and women in sports. The foundation thanked Nichols for her work at the end of the year, saying that, "With Alana at the helm, our virtual programming reached more than two million people, and we awarded more than $800,000 in grants to help girls, community programs, champion athletes, coaches and more unlock the benefits of sports." Alana believes that sports build character and also prepare girls and women for leadership positions in the boardroom. The NCAA found that data from a survey showed "94 percent of the women working in C-suites played sports, and 52 percent played sports at the university level." (Miller, 2018) People working in C-suites are those at high level positions in a company; their job title starts with "chief," such as chief executive officer or chief financial officer.

"I want young women with and without disabilities to dream big, and to have lofty goals, because that's the only way that big things can happen is if you dream them up first."

Alana also works with the High Fives Foundation, founded by her husband, to teach adaptive sports to other athletes.

"I think it's really important to give people with disabilities an outlet to find what they love and then be able to move."

Nichols has also been on the red carpet (nominated for the Best Female Athlete with a Disability ESPY Award) and shook former President Barack Obama's hand at the White House. She still enjoys playing sports and staying involved in community service projects, always being inspired by her family and friends.

BIGGER THAN THE GAME

———

Although I have tried out many different sports from a young age, basketball has been the one that I have played for the longest time. Therefore, it was no surprise to me that I spent a lot of time watching the WNBA (Women's National Basketball Association) games on television. When I was younger and in elementary school, I tried improving my own skills by watching female athletes play and enjoyed seeing competitive games between the teams. However, as I got older and started high school, I realized that the WNBA players I looked up to are so much more than basketball stars on the court. They are also activists, advocates, and athletes using their platforms to drive change in their communities—two players that especially stood out to me were Maya Moore and Renee Montgomery. Moore and Montgomery were also teammates and have won two championships together as players of the Minnesota Lynx, a WNBA team.

"Where Maya goes, championships seem to follow: Maya is a four-time WNBA Champion, six-time WNBA All Star, Olympic Gold Medalist and has won more games than any player in college basketball history." Moore played college basketball at the University of Connecticut and in 2011 was the first overall pick in the WNBA draft. Just a couple of months after entering the league, she helped the Lynx win their first ever championship title in the team's history and was named Rookie of the Year. Her incredible basketball career in the WNBA continued, as she went on to win several Most Valuable Player awards, WNBA championships, Olympic gold medals, and All-Star selections. Maya also became the first female basketball player ever to sign with the Jordan brand. (Maya Moore, 2020)

Throughout her career, Maya has always dedicated time to giving back, showing that she takes on many roles outside of being one of the best WNBA players ever to play the game of basketball. She holds her own basketball camps and clinics for young girls through the "Maya Moore Academy." Not only does she help girls improve their basketball skills, but she also invites speakers, such as coaches, to help the young athletes "enhance personal development" and "focus on leadership and character." (Maya Moore, 2020)

At the age of twenty-nine, in the year 2019, Moore decided to sit out for the WNBA season, despite still being in the peak of her professional career. She wanted to focus on social justice reform, saying that "There are different ways to measure success." (Maya Moore, 2020) I remember reading this story in the news and felt so inspired by her decision to use her platform to drive change in society. Moore sat out from the 2019, 2020, and current 2021 WNBA seasons to work on her campaign, Win With Justice. (Maloney, 2021) She worked to free Jonathan Irons, a man who was wrongly convicted, from prison and engage voters of color in the elections. (Win

With Justice, 2020) This social justice work is so important to Maya for several reasons:

"We feel a responsibility to make the most of our platforms and our privilege by demanding that those around us—those who come to our games to support us, those who voted for us, or those in our neighborhood who have high hopes that we will bring a higher level of thinking to our criminal justice system—are treated with respect, dignity, and fairness." (Win With Justice, 2020)

Renee Montgomery, Maya's former teammate, also sat out during the 2020 season. I remember watching Montgomery play on television and recently interviewed her regarding her journey as a star both on and off the court. Renee shared with me that she started playing basketball when she was really young and fell in love with the sport less than a year after she started playing. She saw her older sisters playing and wanted to follow in their footsteps.

The most important times for Renee during her high school and college sports career were when things were tough: "I had to check myself and look around and see how I could change our situation. So if we weren't winning, I wanted to see what I could do better, or what I could do differently that could help us win." Just like Maya, Renee played college basketball at the University of Connecticut. In 2009, Montgomery was the fourth overall pick in the WNBA draft and was selected by the Minnesota Lynx. This is one of her most memorable experiences as a professional athlete because her parents and college coach were at the draft with her as she began a new journey in her life. She had an incredible WNBA career, winning two championships with the Minnesota Lynx, becoming one of only thirteen players in

WNBA history to make five hundred three-pointers, and being named an All-Star. (Renee Montgomery, 2021)

When I asked Renee about her keys to success, she said, "There's no secret sauce. It's just hard work. I had a crazy work ethic and I was constantly working. And I was constantly figuring out how I could get better. I was ever evolving—in a sense of mentally, too. I watched a lot of film, not just of myself, but of my opponents. I was just trying to find an edge at all times."

In 2020, Montgomery announced that she would be sitting out of the WNBA season. She focused on giving back to the community and fighting for issues she felt strongly about through the Renee Montgomery Foundation. It was founded in 2019 and "strives to promote love, positivity, and equality to all." (Renee Montgomery Foundation, 2021) Renee shared with me that it is important for her to give back because she thinks about all the help she's received along the way: "The people that gave back to me when they didn't even know me, gave me a little piece of advice, just because they saw how eager I was to learn." This not only applies to when she was a young kid but also now as she takes on various roles in the entertainment industry. She explained that she is truly thankful for all the people who have been giving her advice over the years, and she wants to do the same for others: "When it comes to the community work, I want to use my platform, because I was afforded to have one. I want to use that and help people that maybe can't get their voices out and can't get their stories heard, or just want to be a part of something."

The Renee Montgomery Foundation has many initiatives, including The Last Yard. Renee shared that with this initiative, her foundation was fortunate to raise enough funds, even through a pandemic, to give scholarships to two college students. Montgomery is excited to be doing this initiative again with her foundation in the fall. Another campaign that was held through her foundation is the Remember the 3rd initiative, which "was designed to both educate and assist voters heading to the polls during election time." Renee and her foundation also recently participated in the Unity In The Community Back-to-School Backpack Giveaway, where they helped give free backpacks to students. (Renee Montgomery Foundation, 2021)

Montgomery recently retired with the Atlanta Dream of the WNBA in 2021. She continues to spread kindness and is also continuing her career as a sports analyst and TV host. Most recently, Renee made history by becoming a co-owner of her former team, the Atlanta Dream; this made her the first former player to be both an executive and owner of a WNBA team. (WNBA, 2021) Montgomery described this as truly being a dream come true for her. "Breaking barriers for minorities and women by being the first former WNBA player to have both a stake in ownership and a leadership role with the team is an opportunity that I take very seriously." (WNBA, 2021)

WNBA players, like Maya Moore and Renee Montgomery, are true role models to me because they have proven that girls and women are incredible athletes and drive change in their communities at the same time. The Renee Montgomery Foundation exemplifies this with their mission statement that "Moments Equal Momentum": "All it takes is a single moment, a single chance to create momentum. All you need is a second to change everything." (Renee Montgomery Foundation, 2021)

KRISTI YAMAGUCHI

When I spoke to Olympic gold medalist Kristi Yamaguchi, she explained that she found her love for ice skating at a young age. When Kristi was just six years old, she went to watch a local show with her mother at an ice rink in Hayward, California. She was amazed by the gripping performances of the skaters and their vibrant costumes. As the performers glided across the shimmering ice, sparkling lights and instrumental music filled the arena with a magical feeling.

"I fell in love with it [ice skating] then and wanted to try it."

This was just the beginning of Kristi's career. Not only would this moment serve as an inspiration for her athletic journey, but it would also lead to her making a positive impact on others' lives. After attending this magnificent skating show, Kristi knew that she wanted to try ice skating. Her mom took her to the skating rink for the first time when she was six, and that was all it took for Kristi to decide that she wanted to pursue the sport.

"I just kept asking to be taken back to the rink, over and over again."

She started attending practices right away, where she trained and prepared for competitions. Growing up, Kristi drew her motivation from her idol, Dorothy Hamill, and looked up to Hamill's accomplishments. Dorothy was a professional skater and had won the gold medal in the 1976 Winter Olympics for figure skating. She also recalls that Scott Hamilton, who was also an Olympic skater, was another one of her big idols. They eventually became friends, and he is one of Kristi's closest friends to this day. Like her role models, Kristi was determined to become a professional athlete and worked diligently to achieve this goal.

Figure skating is a tough sport and requires many hours of training. It can also be taxing on one's body because of its likelihood of causing injury. It has been reported by Active & Safe that about 80 percent of skaters will suffer an injury from overusing a muscle in their career because they are continuously landing on their ankle when doing jumps and other moves. In addition to figure skating's difficult nature, it is even harder to qualify for the Olympics in this sport. Kristi wanted to compete in the ladies' singles figure skating event, and every year, only three athletes are chosen to represent the United States for this competition. (The Christian Science Monitor, 1992) Despite these potential struggles, Kristi took on the challenge, started her journey to become an Olympian, and never looked back. Even while in fourth grade, Kristi followed a rigorous training schedule. Her coaches expected her to wake up early in the morning and be ready to practice. (Keegan, 2018)

"I was skating almost every day before school and sometimes after school. My bedtime was always around seven thirty, maybe eight at the latest." (Keegan, 2018)

Making commitments and following through on them is never easy, and the fact that Kristi was able to do that at such a young age is truly admirable. Kristi might not have known this at that time, but she had the potential in her to overcome challenges and become an Olympic athlete. She continued training for several hours a day with her coaches and put in the time to become the best figure skater she could be. Kristi started seeing the direct results of her hard work during her high school years. In 1987, she competed in the World Figure Skating Championships in the pairs competition and won a bronze medal. She returned the following year to compete in the pairs and singles competition, winning two gold medals. (Keegan, 2018)

Many athletes who participate in sports, such as figure skating, that require repetitive movements often struggle with burnout and experience fatigue or get overwhelmed. I myself did gymnastics from a young age but decided to stop in fourth grade when I was about to compete on a team. There were training sessions almost every day for about three to four hours and meets on the weekends. I was getting bored of the repetitive movements in gymnastics and felt stressed by the large time commitment it required, so I decided to switch to basketball.

Kristi also faced somewhat similar obstacles during her athletic journey that she had to work hard to overcome. About a year before the Olympics, she hit a mental roadblock because of outside pressures weighing down on her and creating a negative overall feeling. Rather than enjoying the sport she had loved so much from a young age, Kristi felt as if she was just going through the motions of figure skating. One day, a friend of hers that she trained with pulled her aside and said:

"Why are you so miserable? You're making us miserable training with you. You know, you're a great skater, you work hard,
and you're going to become a world champion."

Kristi just laughed, saying that the thought of her becoming
a world champion was "crazy."

Her friend responded, "No, you will. But you know you can
enjoy it, right? You can smile once in a while, like, why are
you skating?"

That one question, "Why are you doing this?" really hit home
for Kristi. She thought about it deeply and tried imagining
how her life would look like without skating.

"I couldn't imagine it," she said. "I knew there were other
things in skating I wanted to accomplish that I didn't want
to just give up."

This moment helped Kristi refocus and think about why she
started skating. She thought about how she could gain back
her passion and love for the sport.

"When I found it, you know, it was just a simple change in
perspective. I quit worrying about how everyone else wanted
me to skate or be like. I said I was going to do what I wanted
to do and had so much more fun doing it that way."

Kristi's positive attitude definitely reflected in her performances. In 1992, she qualified to compete in the Albertville
Winter Olympics for ladies' singles figure skating. She brought
a gold medal home and made history by becoming the first

Asian American to win a gold medal in Olympic figure skating. This also led to her being inducted into the Figure Skating Hall of Fame and US Olympic Hall of Fame. (Tong, 2018)

"It was always an honor to represent our country and compete, knowing that I was one of the best in the country to go out, and wear the stars and stripes."

Yamaguchi credits much of her success to one important value: determination.

"I loved what I did and I had a passion for it, but you have to have a certain amount of determination to get over the challenges, the hurdles, and to be willing to put the extra work in that's needed. Without that [determination], I think it would have been hard to compete at the high level that I did."

Kristi is a true star on and off the ice. In her early twenties, she remembers her parents always telling her how fortunate she was to have things work out the way they did for her and to have the support of her community. After seeing her parents actively volunteering in the community, she was inspired to do the same. She remembers thinking that she wanted to do something to help underserved children.

"I had the support to go after my dreams. I wanted to try to give some kind of support for kids out there to give them the opportunity to go after their dreams, because that's not always the case in every community."

She decided to start the Always Dream Foundation, which initially focused on helping underprivileged communities in the San Francisco Bay Area. In 2011, she redirected the foundation's focus to one specific area: early literacy. At that time, her daughters were seven and five, so naturally early literacy and education were a constant focus. Along with her husband, she was reading a lot of books to her daughters, and they wanted to hear the same books read over and over again. This inspired Kristi to write children's books and eventually become a *New York Times* Bestselling Author. Many of the books she has written teach young children about important values in life, such as kindness, perseverance, embracing differences, and being open to new friendships. She was also motivated to focus her organization's mission on "wanting every child out there to have a book and to be read to."

Since 2011, she has spent a lot of her time promoting early literacy by visiting classrooms, donating tablets and books to families, and reading to young children. There is one especially memorable experience Kristi had with her foundation, which she talks a lot about. During the end of a reading program that Yamaguchi's foundation had done at a school, parents were sharing feedback about what they liked or what could be improved. A father spoke up and said:

"My son never used to like to read before and wasn't really interested in books. But through the program, he discovered books about outer space and the moon, which he wanted to read over and over again. And then soon he discovered other books about other planets and now he wants to be an astronaut."

This experience is unforgettable for Kristi because it is an incredible example of how worlds are opened up to young children through books, and dreams are made possible. Since the start of the Always Dream Foundation in 1996, the organization has served over ten thousand students. (Always-Dream, 2021)

From the start of Kristi's figure skating career at the age of six, to giving the gift of reading to thousands of young children, she has lived her life by following one key principle:

"There's no secret to success. It's just plain and simple hard work."

Kristi Yamaguchi has shown the world that women in sports are determined and capable of making history, winning a gold medal, and being honored in the US Olympic Hall of Fame. She is also an incredible example of how female athletes are working hard to give back to the community and help transform children's dreams into reality.

MELISSA STOCKWELL

—

For Olympic medalist Melissa Stockwell, it has always been about representing the red, white, and blue on the American flag—whether that be as a US Army soldier or as a Paralympian. Her mom recalls that from a young age, Melissa was always jumping and climbing on everything, so she put her daughter in gymnastics at the age of five. When I spoke to Melissa, she mentioned that she enjoyed being in a structured environment where she could get her energy out, and she fell in love with the fortitude necessary to compete in sports. Gymnastics was definitely Stockwell's sport of choice as she was already competing at a high level and dreamed of going to the Olympics.

At a young age, Melissa learned how lucky she was to be living in America and always wanted to give back to her country. She decided to join the US Army because she has "loved the American flag and wanted to wear that [US Army] uniform to represent our country." While serving in the military, Stockwell learned so much about "the camaraderie, teamwork, and putting something above yourself." She also explained that many of the important skills she learned by joining the army carry over into everyday life, like "being on time, how to be part of a team, and how to be disciplined."

I myself have always been inspired by all our country's soldiers' dedication and selflessness. I have written letters of encouragement to troops overseas and always say "thank you for your service" when I meet a member of the US military. However, it was only after interviewing Melissa Stockwell that I truly understood how much courage and perseverance America's army members must have. When I asked her about overcoming hardships, she shared her own powerful story with me: "On April 13, 2004, it was on a routine convoy, while I was serving in central Baghdad. My vehicle was struck by a roadside bomb, which ultimately resulted in the loss of my left leg above the knee."

From there, Stockwell was sent to Walter Reed Army Medical Center, which at the time was where all the wounded soldiers from Iraq and Afghanistan were being treated. At the age of just twenty-four, Melissa had lost her leg in a tragic accident while serving her country. Although this was a difficult challenge she had to face, Stockwell was able to conquer it with great fortitude—the aspect of sports she had always loved. Also, at Walter Reed, she was surrounded by other soldiers who had gone through such similar situations and had experiences that were so unexpected.

"A lot of them [other wounded soldiers] were much worse off than I was. So, if I ever had a moment where I felt bad for myself, all I had to do was look around and see another soldier missing two legs, or their eyesight, or a leg and an arm. I put things in perspective pretty quickly and realized how lucky I was to only have lost one leg. I wanted to live my life as best I could."

At the time when Melissa lost her leg, she didn't even imagine winning an Olympic medal as she was not aware that the Paralympics, which began in 1960, even existed. (International Paralympic Committee, 2021) During her recovery at the hospital, someone put on a presentation about the Paralympics. Stockwell attended this presentation and recalls, "It very much changed my life because I sat there." The presenter shared that if the US Army soldiers dedicated themselves to a sport and beat their competitors in it, then they could compete on the world's biggest athletic stage for someone with a disability. A dream was born pretty quickly and Melissa knew that she wanted to be a Paralympian.

Similar to the hard work and discipline involved in her role as a member of the military, Stockwell put a lot of time and energy into her athletic training. She competed in the 2008 Beijing Paralympics for swim in the one hundred and four hundred freestyles and the one hundred butterfly race. (Triathlon Inspires, 2021) Although Melissa did not win a medal that year, she learned that it was not always about the destination but rather about the journey, which in her case was overcoming the loss of her leg. The participation medal that she received at the end of the games was so meaningful to Melissa, because it taught her the importance of "persevering through things that come your way."

She continued working to achieve her dream. because even though she had qualified for the games, she still wanted to make it onto the podium someday. For the 2016 Rio

Paralympics, Stockwell decided to compete in the triathlon, which incorporates three events (swimming, biking, and running) into one race. She describes being an elite athlete as a full-time job because she would swim every day and alternate between biking and running. Her rigorous schedule also included utilizing strength and sports therapy to ensure that her body was ready for the next day's workout. In total, she trained for more than twenty hours a week.

After overcoming so many challenges and hardships, Melissa's dream of winning an Olympic medal became a reality on September 11, 2016, when she won the bronze medal for the Paralympic triathlon event. She explains that this moment when she accomplished a personal goal of hers will "probably go down as one of the best days of my life." It was incredible for Stockwell to be able to experience this moment with her family.

Outside of her professional athletic career, Melissa is also a motivational speaker, author, and co-founder of an organization called Dare2tri. As one of the co-founders of Dare2tri, an organization that started back in 2011, Stockwell works to involve athletes with physical disabilities in the sport of triathlon. The organization is mainly based out of Chicago and has served over 350 athletes including youth athletes, adults, and injured service members. Dare2tri has helped these athletes in so many different ways, from getting them active in their communities to helping them compete at the Paralympic Games.

"The mission is to provide them with anything and everything that they need to get to the starting line of a triathlon. Our motto is 'one inspires many,' and our athletes do that both on and off the racecourse."

Similar to Melissa's reason for joining the US Army, she takes on various community roles outside of her athletic career because she is passionate about giving back. Stockwell says that she wouldn't be where she is today if it weren't for those who helped her out, so she wants to give back to the next generation and give hope to those who have also gone through traumatic events. As a motivational speaker, she gives a lot of talks about her own story and the power of choice.

"I think when things come our way in life that we don't expect, we have the power to choose how we perceive them and how we deal with them."

In her inspirational talks, she explains this by describing that there is a downhill road of self-pity and wondering "Why me?" but there is also an uphill road. The uphill road is a little bit harder, but when you choose to accept whatever happened and surround yourself with the key people that want you to get better and improve, it's amazing how much you can do. Stockwell mentioned that "a lot of times you end up even better on the other [uphill road] side."

Her book, *The Power of Choice: My Journey from Wounded Warrior to World Champion*, was published on August 4, 2020. She aims to share her story with others and inspire the people who read her book.

"They [the readers of her book] think about their own life and realize the path that they've taken and realize that they can get out there and make their life what they want it to be."

Melissa Stockwell's journey to success has never been easy, but with her passion and dedication, she has become a role model for so many others. She has also proven that women can be brave in overcoming challenges as she herself is a US Army war veteran, Paralympic bronze medalist, and so much more.

LINDSEY VONN

Lindsey Vonn is widely known as being the best female alpine ski racer of all time. She has four women's World Cup overall championships, three Olympic medals, and eight World Championship medals, and she has the most World Cup race wins for any female, with eighty-two victories. (Encyclopedia Britannica Online Ed, 2021) However, her journey to success has never been easy as she has endured many skiing accidents, crashes, and threatening injuries. At the end of her illustrious career, when she retired in 2019, an opinion article from *The Washington Post* by Louis Meyers said, "Many years from now—long after the cheering has died away—the mountains will remember her [Lindsey Vonn]." Vonn commented on this statement during a 2019 interview with the morning news show *TODAY*'s Hoda Kotb: "I hope that I've done something in my career that's more meaningful than eighty-two wins, and I hope that the mountains remember me. I definitely know that the fences will."

At the age of just two, Lindsey was introduced to alpine ski racing by her family members. She recalls that growing up, her family had a passion for skiing, starting with her grandfather.

When I asked her how she discovered her love for the sport, she answered, "Although I tried figure skating, gymnastics, and soccer, none of them stuck. I realized my love for skiing at an early age (it was also what I was best at) and never looked back." She started attending international events at the early age of nine and by her teenage years, she was already making history and winning World Cup points. She also won her first World Cup race and started participating in competitions with the best alpine ski racers in the world. (Red Bull, 2012)

In 2006, Vonn suffered several injuries, including bone bruising and a pulled tendon. However, rather than letting those setbacks bring her down, she used them as motivation to work even harder: "Setbacks motivate me," she says. Despite her injuries, Lindsey was still able to get some wins at the 2006 World Championship. The following season, she came back stronger than ever and achieved her childhood goal of winning an Overall World Cup. 2010 was also a special year because Vonn became an Olympic champion at the Vancouver Games and the first ever American woman to win an Olympic gold medal in the downhill. She also won back-to-back ESPY (Excellence in Sports Performance) awards in 2010 and 2011 for Best Female Athlete. During the 2011-12 season, Lindsey inched closer to becoming the woman with the most World Cup race victories as she ranked third with fifty-three wins. (Red Bull, 2012)

She faced another challenge that disrupted her next season, as she injured her knee in 2013 while skiing in Austria and was flown back to the US to have surgery. After focusing on rehabilitation for six months, Vonn got back onto the ski mountain, but she unfortunately experienced the toughest season in her career. She explains that while she was skiing, her knee "completely gave out." She suffered a serious tear to her ligament and was forced to miss the 2014 Winter Olympics in Sochi. As always, Vonn stayed determined, and the following season was not only a comeback season, but also one in which she made history. She surpassed the record that was set then of sixty-two World Cup wins and successfully became the female alpine ski racer with the most World Cup race victories. Lindsey was officially named the best female skier to ever play the sport and celebrated this historic moment with her family. (Red Bull, 2012)

She started the next year with a newfound strength and several wins. However, once again, her season was cut short because of injuries. After severely crashing, a rescue sledge brought her off the mountain and took her to the hospital. Since Lindsey was initially diagnosed with a hairline fracture at her knee, she competed the next day. However, after another examination, she discovered that she had actually suffered a triple fracture. Making one of the most difficult decisions of her career, Vonn decided to end her season early. (Red Bull, 2012)

From personal experience, I know that watching from the sidelines is never easy. I myself broke my wrist in sixth grade while playing basketball and had to sit out for the first half of the season. It is definitely difficult to not be able to play a sport that you've loved for so long, and it is even harder to get back to your normal state of play after recovering from an injury.

From 2016 to 2018, Lindsey also injured other parts of her body while skiing, which included breaking her arm and injuring her back, amid continuous knee pain. However, she was still able to compete in the 2018 Winter Olympics in Pyeongchang and even won a bronze medal. The 2018 to 2019 season would be Lindsey's final one because of her injuries. She wrote in an Instagram post, "My body is broken beyond repair and it isn't letting me have the final season I dreamed of. My body is screaming at me to stop and it's time for me to listen." (@LindseyVonn, February 1, 2019)

I see Vonn as personifying perseverance because of her determination to not only become the best athlete she could be, but also to better the sports sphere for all girls and women. Much like women who had to fight for their right to vote, Lindsey kept getting on the horse and giving it everything she had. If our sisters hadn't done the same, our lives would be much different today, just as the sports world would be much different without Vonn's perseverance. When Lindsey won bronze in the 2018 Winter Olympics, twenty-four million viewers watched, and "it was the first Olympics in which prime time coverage of women's sports eclipsed that devoted to men." (McManus, 2019)

When asked about her most memorable experiences from her professional sports career, she mentioned: "All of my Olympic experiences were special. From winning gold in Vancouver to getting third in Pyeongchang and the significance of that after my grandfather's death. I will also cherish my bronze medal from my last race in Are, Sweden. There's always a backstory to the wins, whether it's coming back from injury or what I was going through in my life that makes each victory special to me." In an interview with CNN, Lindsey further explained that her grandfather always supported her throughout her journey and if it weren't for him, she wouldn't be racing. (Hodgetts, 2018)

Outside of her sports career, Lindsey Vonn is also an author of two books; one of her books, *Rise: My Story*, is still in the works, and the other one, *Strong is the New Beautiful*, was published in 2016. She explains her purpose for writing this book: "*Strong is the New Beautiful* was really special because I got to share what a healthy lifestyle as an athlete looks like and also how to grow confidence from within yourself and not look for that acceptance from anyone else."

She is also the founder of the Lindsey Vonn Foundation, which works to empower young girls: "My Foundation is very special to me. I want that [Lindsey Vonn Foundation] to be part of my legacy—not just skiing." Her foundation awards scholarships and also holds camps for young girls that are centered around fostering self-confidence and making new friends. Vonn meets the girls attending the camp and speaks to them about important topics, like staying positive: "Something that I've always had trouble with, especially when I was your age, was staying positive. A lot of people told me that I couldn't do it or that I wasn't good enough. I had a season where I didn't finish in fifty out of fifty-five races. These lessons that you are learning today [at the camp] help you get through that easier, and I wish I had that when I was your age because it was definitely a tough road. Staying positive, while it isn't easy, it's really important." (Lindsey Vonn Foundation, 2021)

The impact that Lindsey has made on the lives of young girls is evident. One of the girls that attended her camp said that she learned: "No matter the situation, you can always think of the positive things versus the negative. I just have to love myself." (Lindsey Vonn Foundation, 2021) Other girls have said they have learned how to be confident because everyone is beautiful in their own way: "I can do anything! My body is my machine and it's beautiful. My limits are only in my head, and I can get through them." (Lindsey Vonn Foundation, 2021)

When I asked Lindsey for one piece of advice she would give, she answered: "Probably the hardest thing I've had to learn and the advice I would give young female athletes is to invest and believe in yourself. It is a big cliché, but having that mentality was a big key to my success. It's not easy, but you always need to keep pushing yourself."

Vonn has not only made an impact on alpine skiing by becoming the best female skier of all time but has also used her platform to give back to the community. Through her foundation, she has inspired young girls to be strong and believe in themselves and continues to do so to this day.

KENDALL COYNE SCHOFIELD

———

Kendall Coyne Schofield represents the new face of women's ice hockey.

"I need the sport," Kendall said in her small, toddler voice to her parents. Her mom responded, "You're three. How do you—" "I want to do what Kevin is doing," she said. Kendall's parents had signed her older brother, Kevin, up for hockey and had put Kendall in figure skating. She did the sport for barely a week before telling her parents that she wanted to do what her brother was doing, which was ice hockey. (As Fast as Her: Chicago Blackhawks, 2020)

Kendall shared with me that growing up, she looked up to her role model, Cammi Granato, an American professional ice hockey player. When Kendall was seven years old, she attended Cammi's hockey camp with over one hundred other girls. This was right after the 1998 Olympic Games, so Granato had her gold medal with her that she had recently won.

"I remember the feeling of empowerment Cammi gave me as a little girl that day and every day forward, a feeling of a superpower that I could accomplish anything I set my mind to. At that point, everyone told me girls don't belong in hockey. And that day I realized—they did."

When Kendall went home after attending this camp, she turned to her parents and said, "I want to go to the Olympics."

Similar to her role model, Cammi, Kendall's journey to becoming an Olympian was nowhere near easy.

Since there weren't many other girls that were Kendall's age playing ice hockey at the time, she was often the only girl on an all-boys team. Her mom remembers constantly hearing rude comments from other parents, like "Hit her, take her out" and "She's horrible. She's a girl." Kendall also felt a sense of loneliness being the only girl on the team, especially before the games when she saw the rest of her teammates going into the locker room and having a good time, while she went into a storage closet by herself. (As Fast as Her: Chicago Blackhawks, 2020)

When I was younger, I also had experiences when I was one of the few girls in a camp or on a basketball team. However, I always had a locker room that I could use, and I can't even imagine having to go inside a storage closet, like Kendall had to do at such a young age. Maybe I wouldn't have played on the team or participated in the camp anymore. Kendall did in fact think of quitting ice hockey when she faced these difficult obstacles.

"There was a time in my youth career that I thought about quitting hockey, because I was getting made fun of. Getting called a tomboy. Getting told to go do what normal girls do, and you don't belong. And getting cut from teams because I was a girl." (As Fast as Her: Chicago Blackhawks, 2020)

Facing these tough challenges is never easy and is especially difficult when you have to face them at such a young age like Kendall did. However, Kendall persevered and did not let anyone come in the way of achieving her dreams. She shared with me how she was able to rise to the challenge and play the sport she loved most.

"I overcame these things by always remembering why I play the game, and that is because I love it. No matter how many times people tried to chase me out of the game, they couldn't diminish the love I had for the game, and that showed every time I stepped on the ice."

As Kendall continued developing her skills in ice hockey, she made a high-level hockey boys' team and played with boys who were a year older than her. One of her childhood teammates from this team remembers that Kendall's work ethic was evident right away—she was always in the gym doing extra workouts and drills.

"It was almost like she was a rink manager, and she pretty much worked at the rink. I wouldn't be surprised if she had a key," he recalls. (As Fast as Her: Chicago Blackhawks, 2020)

While playing on this team, Kendall's teammates made her realize that it was possible for her to be accepted as a hockey player. Rather than seeing gender, they saw Kendall as a talented player and valuable member of the team who was there to improve her game.

At the age of fifteen, Kendall went to a national girls' ice hockey camp. She came home so motivated from this camp and knew that she had to make the National Olympic Team. (Kendall Coyne, 2020)

A couple years later, Kendall started playing college-level ice hockey at Northeastern University. There, she became a part of the first Northeastern women's team to qualify for the NCAA Tournament in program history.

In 2011, Kendall became a part of the US Women's National Team, where she went on to become a six-time World Champion. She also played in the 2014 Olympic Winter Games, where she won a silver medal, and in the 2018 Olympic Winter Games, where she won gold. Although it may seem like Kendall reached the peak of her career by achieving her main goals by playing on the National Team and winning an Olympic medal, she actually made history on January 25, 2019. (Kendall Coyne, 2020)

The NHL, National Hockey League, had invited Kendall to demonstrate a drill at the All-Star Weekend. The NHL All-Star Skills Competition is an annual event where the best ice hockey players are invited to compete in various events. One of these events is the Fastest Skater Competition, in which the player has to skate around the ice rink as fast as they can. Right before the start of this event in 2019, one of the players who was supposed to participate in the competition got injured. (As Fast as Her: Chicago Blackhawks, 2020)

Four hours before the competition started, Kendall got a phone call that said, "You are going to be the first woman to compete in the NHL All-Star Skills Competition." (She Breaks Barriers: Kendall Coyne Schofield, 2019) She remembers almost falling over when she got this call, before rushing to take a shower and going to the rink to prepare for the Fastest Skater Competition. (As Fast as Her: Chicago Blackhawks, 2020)

When Kendall got to the starting line, she felt a sense of excitement because she knew that this was her opportunity to break down barriers, open doors to new opportunities, and make a lasting impact on women's sports. She also felt pressured because she was aware that if she fell down or stumbled during the race, the story would become "I told you so. The women don't belong." (She Breaks Barriers: Kendall Coyne Schofield, 2019) The thoughts running through her head at that moment were:

"You have the weight of the sport on your shoulders right now. And really embrace this moment, enjoy this moment. And prove to the world that women belong in the sport of hockey." (As Fast as Her: Chicago Blackhawks, 2020)

Right when the whistle blew, Kendall took off. The other players and fans looked at her in awe as she proved to the entire world that female ice hockey players are fast skaters too. She recalls that as she skated around the rink, everything was a blur and she reminded herself, "Move your legs as fast as they can go. They're not very long, but just move them like you know how to." (As Fast as Her: Chicago Blackhawks, 2020)

Kendall reached the finish line 14.346 seconds later, less than a second later than the fastest skater in the NHL. She completed the race smoothly and became the first woman to compete in the NHL All-Star Skills Competition. (Benjamin, 2019)

She explained, "It was a moment that proved women belong in the sport of ice hockey and a moment that all of us have worked so hard for. That's the moment you dream about." (She Breaks Barriers: Kendall Coyne Schofield, 2019)

This moment not only broke a barrier in the sport of hockey, but it also showed the importance of visibility. Many people have the false perception that female hockey players are slower than male hockey players. For Kendall to compete in the NHL All-Star Skills Competition proved that women belong in the sport of ice hockey and are equally entertaining to watch as men ice hockey players.

Off the ice, Kendall focuses her time on giving back to the community and mentoring young girls, like Cammi did for her.

"Hockey has brought me so many incredible experiences I never would've dreamed of when I was three years old, and I put on figure skates. Now that I've been able to accomplish that, my mission is to leave the game better than it was." (As Fast as Her: Chicago Blackhawks, 2020)

Kendall has seen, felt, and lived through moments where having a visible role model can change your life forever. She remembers being inspired by Cammi when she attended her hockey camp at the age of seven. Kendall hopes to inspire the next generation of girls in ice hockey and change their lives through her own Annual Kendall Coyne Hockey Camp. Being a role model requires a lot of dedication and responsibility, but it is truly important to Kendall.

"To see the smiles on the kids' faces, to hear how much they love the game, to see them year after year, and watch them grow—it's so worth it. To see the amount of girls playing, I can't put it into words." (As Fast as Her: Chicago Blackhawks, 2020)

From being the only girl on an all-boys ice hockey team, to being lonely at the rinks her entire childhood, it is truly special for Kendall to see so many girls attend her hockey camp and watch the sport of women's ice hockey grow. USA Hockey has reported that over the past ten years, participation in women's ice hockey has grown by 34 percent.

"It shows that we're worth something. Cammi heard she wasn't worth anything. I've heard I'm not worth anything. I think I continue to fight, and play this game so that these little girls aren't told they're not worth anything." (As Fast as Her: Chicago Blackhawks, 2020)

Kendall also advocates for women's sports and works to change the way that most of the media currently perceives female athletes. At the 2019 espnW Summit in NYC, she spoke on a panel regarding female athletes' fight for equal respect and explained why female ice hockey players struggle to gain recognition: "Where we struggle is that people want to see our face. And we wear a cage. So how are we relevant to that marketer, because all the consumer wants to see is how pretty you are. Not how good of an athlete you are." (As Fast as Her: Chicago Blackhawks, 2020)

She is working to change the way consumers view female athletes and often speaks about how focusing on the sports highlights of these athletes for marketing will hopefully increase the media coverage female ice hockey players receive.

Kendall is a champion for women's sports and has definitely proven to the entire world that women belong to the sport of ice hockey. She wants all athletes to know to:

"Always believe in yourself, follow your dreams, and be willing to put in the work it takes to accomplish your dreams."

She currently lives with her husband, Michael Schofield, who is a football player, and together they give back to various communities through their Schofield Family Foundation.

Not only has Kendall competed in the NHL All-Star Skills Competition, but she has also furthered her career in the NHL by starting her broadcasting and coaching career. She was a commentator for the San Jose Sharks and recently became the first woman to be a player development coach for the Chicago Blackhawks, an NHL team, in the team's ninety-four-year history. (Myers, 2020)

Kendall has already changed the landscape of women's ice hockey forever. She continues to inspire the next generation of athletes and passionately advocates for female athletes' fight for equal pay, media coverage, and respect.

LAUREN FISHER

—

As many younger siblings, like myself, would do, Lauren Fisher followed in the footsteps of her three older brothers growing up. However, she also had a determined mind of her own, like many of the women in this book. She played several sports, like her brothers, and competed in workouts with her dad. A 2020 documentary called "Growing Up Strong: Lauren Fisher" shared that when her brothers' friends came over and all of them would be playing outside, Lauren would get thrown around and come cry to her mom about it, who would respond:

"Lauren, if you want to play with them, just quit crying and go out there."

Lauren would wipe her tears and continue playing, never giving up. Her brother even said that "she hates losing the most out of everybody in the family and is definitely the most competitive one." (Growing Up Strong: Lauren Fisher, 2020) From a young age, it was evident that she had the mental and physical drive needed to become a successful athlete. Lauren shared with me that when she was thirteen years old, she wanted to improve her strength for basketball, and after seeing her brothers doing CrossFit, she decided to try it out too. CrossFit involves a combination of cardio, weightlifting, and gymnastics movements. After trying her first workout, she knew that CrossFit was the one sport she wanted to pursue for the rest of her life. Lauren evolved from a young child competing in workouts with her dad to a professional CrossFit athlete.

I was able to connect with Lauren's story right away because I also started CrossFit during my freshman year of high school to prepare for my basketball season. Initially, I was a little hesitant to go, but I decided to try it out since my brother was doing it too. At the time, I wasn't too interested in the weightlifting aspect of CrossFit. I never enjoyed going to basketball strengthening sessions, however, after finishing my first year of CrossFit, I decided to make it my main sport. I became friends with many of the other athletes and coaches at the gym and started to love the weightlifting part of CrossFit too. I gradually started gaining strength, lifting more weight, and even breaking my personal records. Every day when I went to the training sessions, I looked forward to doing the workout and cheering on the other athletes too.

Lauren shared with me that her CrossFit journey was especially challenging when she first started the sport.

"I was made fun of by the other guys for being too muscular and bulky. They made fun of me for doing CrossFit, because at the time, it wasn't very normal for girls to be doing it."

Although it is not always easy to ignore what others think of you, Lauren did not let other people's opinions stop her from pursuing her passion and participating in the sport she enjoyed most. I believe that she made the right decision by only listening to the people who truly love and care for her, like her father.

"I learned to not listen to them [other people] and just ignore them. My dad taught me to not follow the crowd and not do what everyone else is doing, to kind of be your own leader. Because if you try to follow what everyone else is doing, you are just going to conform to what they want you to do, rather than actually doing what you were put into this world to do."

Living by her father's philosophy of being your own leader, Lauren was able to work toward her goal of qualifying for the CrossFit Games. The CrossFit Games is a yearly competition in which athletes across the globe compete in various CrossFit workouts to earn the title of "Fittest on Earth." (CrossFit LLC, 2021) Once Lauren had made up her mind that she wanted to go to the Games, there wasn't anything that would stop her from doing so.

The 2020 documentary covering Lauren's inspiring story shared that in the beginning, when she first qualified for professional CrossFit competitions, Lauren went against ladies who were much older than her. Even though her competitors had been doing the sport for many years, she was motivated to work even harder when she didn't perform too well in an event. Her coach recalls, "You could tell that it was bothering her, but not in a demotivating way. It was bothering her in a way like 'I'm not going to let this happen again.'" (Growing Up Strong: Lauren Fisher, 2020) Once again, her dad's belief of being your own leader guided her onto the route to success.

"My dad used to always say, 'We can be whoever we want to be, we just have to work harder than everyone else.'" (Growing Up Strong: Lauren Fisher, 2020)

Lauren implemented her father's advice in her own CrossFit journey. As a college student, she balanced her academics with her athletic career and never missed a single training session. (Growing Up Strong: Lauren Fisher, 2020) In 2013, Lauren's determination and willingness to overcome challenges was made evident to the rest of the world. She qualified for the 2013 CrossFit Games and continued to do so for the next six years. In 2014, Lauren placed ninth in the entire world for the title of Fittest Woman on Earth at the age of twenty! (Growing Up Strong: Lauren Fisher, 2020)

However, as it was in her childhood and high school years, Lauren's professional CrossFit journey has never been easy. In 2015, she sprained her ankle but continued to compete on it for a whole year. Immediately after the games in 2016, Lauren realized that something wasn't right with her ankle and decided to get an MRI.

"I found out that I had a torn tendon, so I needed major ankle surgery, which would put me out for like four to five months from my normal training."

As it is for most athletes battling an injury, this was a tough time for Lauren as she was unable to train and participate in competitions. It is both physically and mentally difficult for athletes to be injured, and a great deal of resilience and commitment is needed during the recovery process. (Quinn, 2020)

Lauren was able to persevere as she had done before and won her way back to the CrossFit Games podium with her team in 2019. She shared that her "highlights so far of being a CrossFit athlete have been going to the games seven times in a row from 2013 to 2019, placing ninth in the entire world in 2014, and winning third place with my team in 2019."

In addition to competing in the CrossFit Games, Lauren has used her story of determination and overcoming challenges to advocate for other girls and women to be confident in their bodies. She draws her inspiration from the experience she had in high school when the guys made fun of her for being too "muscular" and "bulky."

"I know that there are so many girls out there who are also struggling with those same issues and don't know how to deal with it. That's what inspired me to help inspire other women to be okay, to love their bodies, and to feel confident."

Lauren hopes that girls can understand that "being strong can carry over to all aspects of life and make you happier, healthier and more confident." Having survived several years of high school myself, I know that these are words that all young girls need to hear at some point in their lives and truly recognize the importance of being proud of themselves. In Thrive Global, author, business owner, and life coach Jolin Tzeng highlights that every girl and woman needs to have self-confidence because it increases self-worth, allows you to stand up for yourself, and gives you an opportunity to be a role model to others. Tzeng emphasized that "self-confidence allows you to conquer the world. It will help you achieve more than you can imagine."

Lauren grew up with three older brothers, who constantly pushed her around and made her tougher in the process. Her journey to growing up strong, along with the challenges she faced as a female CrossFit athlete, inspired her to start a program that is best described as her life's motto. Lauren founded Grown Strong with the main goal of "challenging women to tap into their individual strength to see that strong is beautiful and giving up is simply not an option." (Grown Strong, 2021) She goes beyond designing workouts for athletes and having a membership program by creating a supportive community to help each person achieve their goal. Lauren also writes blogs, which she shares on the Grown Strong website, regarding topics such as nutrition, training and strengthening for female athletes, and workout motivation. Grown Strong also has its own business line that sells workout clothes for women and nutrition products. Lauren's "relentless pursuit of challenging women is what has created a community crafted by discipline." (Grown Strong, 2021) Lauren shared with me her goal of inspiring others:

"I want to inspire other women to overcome obstacles and to learn that you can be strong, not just physically inside a gym, but also mentally and emotionally in all aspects of life."

She says that she wants young girls and women all around the world to stay strong and confident in themselves and be proud of who they are.

REVOLUTIONIZING WOMEN'S SOCCER

———

During the summer of 1999, more than ninety thousand sports fans had gathered at the Rose Bowl in Pasadena, California, in about one hundred-degree weather, to watch the final game of the Women's World Cup. The United States Women's National Soccer Team was facing off against China in what would become a revolutionary and historic moment in women's sports. I had the incredible opportunity to speak with Brandi Chastain, who was a part of the US Women's National Team that helped bring awareness to and advance girls and women's sports with their unforgettable victory in 1999. (Timm-Garcia, 2019)

Brandi has been active and outgoing from a young age and always enjoyed playing every sport possible. She fell in love with soccer the first time she kicked the ball as she recalls, "When I signed up for soccer and went to my practice for the first time, there was just this lightning bolt of, 'Wow. This is something totally different. I've never experienced this before.'

And it just felt right." Some of Chastain's most important moments from playing soccer in high school were not necessarily on the field, but rather the life lessons she learned from playing sports. Probably the most important lesson was that soccer taught her how to be resilient, because you're going to fall down a lot, so it is important to know how to get back up.

In college, she unfortunately suffered from two ACL injuries, causing her to be out of collegiate soccer for two and a half years. Although it is always difficult to sit out from the sport you love the most, Brandi explained that during the time she was recovering, she learned what it meant to truly be a teammate, as she had always been the starting player on her team: "It was a great perspective builder and a great way for me to learn more about myself. And so I turned a really negative situation into a positive one."

Chastain went on to have a memorable and impactful career as a professional soccer player, becoming an Olympic gold medalist and World Cup champion. Her most memorable experiences were spending time with her teammates, who are like her sisters because they all went through life's moments together: "Of course winning gold medals for the first time and winning World Cups for the first time, those are obviously standout moments, but it's more the personal, off-the-field things that were the glue to what we were doing." These experiences bonded Brandi and her teammates in a way that makes their group truly special.

Among her teammates who competed with Team USA in the iconic 1999 Women's World Cup were Mia Hamm, Julie Foudy, and Michelle Akers. The US Women's National Team had made it to the final round of the tournament and were up against China's women's soccer team while approximately forty million people watched the game on TV in America. (Timm-Garcia, 2019) Even today, this game still holds the "record for largest attendance ever to witness a women's soccer match." (Timm-Garcia, 2019)

It was 120 minutes into the last game of the World Cup and the score was still tied, forcing the game to be decided by penalty kicks. When Brandi was called up for her turn, the two teams had both made four penalty kicks. China was four of five as the third kick was blocked by Team USA's goalkeeper, Briana Scurry. The US women's team had made all four penalty kicks, and Chastain was about to take the last one remaining that would win the game. (Timm-Garcia, 2019) She remembers that she had already gone through the nervous part of contemplating what could happen or what should happen at the beginning of the game when the whistle blew. Brandi mentioned that during this last portion of the game, she was "trying to stay in the moment about where we were at that time, and just do the job that you needed to do."

Right when the soccer ball was kicked by Brandi and hit the back of the net, the stadium erupted in cheers and applause. The United States Women's National Soccer Team had officially won the 1999 Women's World Cup. The celebration that followed became one of the most iconic moments in the history of women's sports. Chastain ripped off her shirt, fell to her knees, and put her hands up in the air. Her teammates sprinted toward her, and the fans joined the players in screaming and celebrating this unforgettable victory. Besides winning, this moment also inspired young girls and uplifted women's sports around the globe by proving that female athletes are very skilled and play at a highly competitive level, just like their male counterparts.

When I asked Brandi how she felt about her kick making such an impact, she defined it as being humbling. Going into the game, the team did not know how big of a difference their win would make but were only slightly aware of the fact that the future of women's soccer in our country, and maybe even around the world, was a little bit on the line. She explained, "When you do something that big, what you hope is that there's a lasting impression made, and that the next time it won't be so hard." This win brought more awareness to the fact that women should have this platform to showcase their athletic abilities, something Brandi and her teammates have always been fighting for: "This was a reasonable, if not even more so than that, situation. For so long we had been fighting an anonymous fight. We all love soccer and we wanted it to grow."

Although I was not yet born when this remarkable game took place, I have watched the replay of the match and of Brandi's penalty kick followed by the iconic celebration several times. Every time I watch the recording of this game, it feels as if I'm actually sitting in the stadium, because you can almost sense the excitement and passion from the screen! I also feel grateful that Chastain and all her teammates left the playing field better than they had found it, for other girls in sports, like myself.

The 1999 US Women's Soccer Team has been named the "'99ers" for the impact they have made on women's sports. Alex Morgan, a current star on the USWNT, shared in an interview that, "All of us look at these '99ers' and the fact that they paved the way so much and we are so grateful for what they did in the sport for us, and now it's up to us to continue to pave that way and give even more opportunities to that next generation." (FIFA, 2019)

The sports bra that Brandi wore when scoring the game winning penalty kick has become a souvenir in the field of girls and women's sports! It is currently framed in Chastain's house, and she is also in the process of speaking with the Smithsonian to display it in the exhibit at the Museum of American History for a while! Also, the picture taken of Brandi's iconic celebration upon scoring the penalty kick appeared on many magazine covers in 1999 and continues to be a face of female athletics.

Historic moments like the 1999 US Women's World Cup win continue to play a role in women's sports today. Now, women's soccer, basketball, gymnastics, and many other sports are being showcased on television more often. Although Brandi and her teammates were not aware of the long-lasting impact their win would make, they are definitely seeing it play out right now. Chastain says that she is celebrating the advancement of women's sports today because it should have happened a long time ago.

The drive now is not just to push for women's soccer as being twenty-four women on a roster with three coaches, but also showcase front office staff, a media platform, and a professional sports environment. Brandi, who is currently working to build a NWSL (National Women's Soccer League) team for the Bay Area, explained that women's soccer currently has more potential that it has ever had before.

As a leader in women's sports, Chastain continues to inspire the next generation of female athletes. In 2005, she co-founded the Bay Area Women's Sports Initiative, BAWSI (pronounced "bossy"), with her teammate who also played in the 1999 Women's World Cup, Julie Foudy, and sports executive Marlene Bjornsrud. The nonprofit organization has been serving the Bay Area since then and aims to "mobilize the women's sports community to engage, inspire, and empower the children who need us the most." (BAWSI, 2020) Brandi feels "that every young girl should have the platform to explore, express, and have an adventure through an athletic lens, no matter their culture, background, or how much money they have. We should all give so that these young girls have a chance to become the people that they want to become, and I think sports is a great place to learn valuable lessons about life."

I also spoke with Dr. Dana Weintraub, who is a co-CEO of BAWSI and pediatrician and previously played collegiate soccer. She shared that while BAWSI is proud of having served over twenty thousand children in the past sixteen years, BAWSI's current focus is on program expansion to middle and high school. Despite the extensive research of the positive benefits of sports on physical and mental health and team sports being one of the most powerful tools for leadership development, too many girls still do not have the opportunity to play.

Dr. Weintraub further explained that "whether or not the historic disparity in opportunity for girls' sports participation is a cause of the lack of women in leadership positions, it is certainly a solution. We hope our programs provide pathways for a generation of leaders reflective of our community and strengthening our community."

Brandi also shared an unforgettable experience with me that she had almost fifteen years ago while coaching a BAWSI camp. She asked all the girls to come huddle at the center of the playground, which she calls the "virtual locker room." She shared that at BAWSI, "We are assertive, push our limits, encourage each other to be awesome, and are unafraid to be our best." Since it was a little quiet, Brandi asked if any of the girls had a celebration or cheer that they wanted to do with the rest of the girls. One girl raised her hand, so Brandi called her to the center of the circle. The girl froze, so Brandi offered to show her celebration moment first, which might help out. Chastain showed the girls how she celebrated when scoring her penalty kick in 1999 and although the girls politely clapped, they didn't get super excited.

When it was the girl's turn again to do her celebration or cheer, what she did was absolutely awesome! Brandi shared that "she did this like gymnastics, back handspring, cartwheel, flip thing that was amazing and she landed it perfectly." The girls went berserk, and it was incredible as Brandi told them, "Now that's being bossy! Now go back out there and play like you mean it!" After the day was over and everyone was picking up their backpacks, Brandi felt a tug on her sleeve, and it was the girl from the middle of the circle: "She looked up at me with these big brown eyes I'll never forget and she said, 'Thank you for not giving up on me.' It brings tears to my eyes even today because I think about how simple it was to stand next to her, to encourage her to go for it, and to support her."

Chastain mentioned that the little girl's greatness had nothing to do with her, but the confidence that she felt when she had advocacy was palpable to her: "That has been, for me, the foundation of what BAWSI is, and it's giving a platform to young girls to be whoever it is that they want to be and then to celebrate them."

HILARY KNIGHT

—

Hilary Knight is arguably the best female ice hockey player in the world. When I spoke with Hilary, she shared that since she comes from a huge game family, in which many of her cousins are national level skiers, she was on skis at the age of just two! Moving away from the mountains in northern California to the Midwest, Knight was introduced to the game of ice hockey, which was quite popular among the kids in her community. Growing up, she focused on having fun playing hockey and appreciating all the good things that come out of sports. However, she faced many challenges being a girl playing what was then considered a male-dominated sport. Knight shared that she was "left off of teams that I should have been a part of, because I was a girl, and I was taking a spot away from somebody's son or another boy on the roster." Hilary's love for ice hockey and passion to grow the game motivated her to overcome these obstacles and compete at a high level.

A key part of her success as a professional athlete came from having a vision, understanding she had a dream, and figuring out how she would reach her goals. Knight played ice hockey at the University of Wisconsin and went on to become an Olympian with the United States Women's National Ice Hockey Team, winning two silver medals, in the 2010 and 2014 Winter Olympics. (Team USA, 2021) In the 2018 Winter Olympics, Hilary Knight and Team USA beat Canada to win the Olympic gold medal—the first one for the US Women's Ice Hockey Team in twenty years! This was such a memorable moment as right after the team had won the game, "gloves and sticks flew all over the place, American flags waved, tears streamed down the players' faces and Team USA embraced the moment with its most significant group hug on the ice in twenty years." (Rosen, 2018) In our conversation, Hilary mentioned, "It's such a special moment to share with one another, because you understand the hard work that you've put in, the vision you've had when you were a child, and then all the people that were along the way supporting you."

In addition to winning medals, one of Knight's most memorable experiences has been the equitable support battle when the team boycotted the 2017 World Championships because they were not receiving fair treatment and pay. They eventually were able to reach an agreement and make a deal before the championships, so they agreed to play in the tournament again. (Howard, 2017) The ice hockey star recalls, "We established a foundation or mark point to move forward in our sport and provide more resources and try to promote the growth of women's hockey." The team put countless hours into this fight, and this is just part of the beginning of their journey to advance the game. They couldn't have written a better story, as the team showed up to the World Championships after speaking out on the unfair treatment they were facing and returned home with a win!

Knight is truly dedicated to creating more opportunities for young girls and women to play sports and being a role model for them. In 2014, she practiced with the Anaheim Ducks of the NHL (National Hockey League), making her the first female non-goalie to practice with an NHL Team. (Associated Press, 2014) She set a clear example for so many other women that they can play the sport of ice hockey at a highly competitive level too. Hilary did mention that although it is unfortunate that there aren't many opportunities now, times are definitely changing. She is inspiring the next generation of female athletes, and Knight said it best: "It's just one of these things where it's like if she could see it, she can be it. We're just another piece in the puzzle, as we move this sport forward and as we move women in this industry forward. If not now, then when?"

These issues that Hilary advocates to solve are so important to her because many of them resonate with her and are experiences that she's lived through. Knight has worked so hard to establish this amazing platform and she wants to use it to give a voice to other people: "Whether it's speaking out on body image, equal pay, or diversity and inclusion, there's so much to do. We all know the value of sport and how beautiful sport can be in individuals' lives, and if there's a way to weave in an empowering message or shine light on some positivity, that's what I aim to do." All her teammates also believe that their social impact pieces are equally important to their successes on the ice.

In the future, Knight would love to see the game of women's ice hockey grow with a professional league and a platform that consistently covers their games so that fans can tune in.

She also hopes to make the beautiful sport more accessible to everyone. Knowing Hilary, she is quick to speak up when she sees an inequity present and actively works to create equal opportunities for all. In a 2020 interview with Haley Rosen of *Just Women's Sports*, she spoke about the challenges female athletes in the NWHL (National Women's Hockey League) had been facing since the league was created in 2015: "Whether it was our athletes not getting paid or not having the resources we needed, or a bus showing up three hours late, or a bus not having a bathroom when we're traveling from Boston to Buffalo—these were all slaps in the face that kept adding up."

I was so disappointed when I read this, because I could never imagine professional athletes having to deal with these kinds of issues—they should be able to focus on their game and not have to worry about fighting for equality and basic rights—it should already be given.

However, Hilary is part of a group that is paving the way for the future of women's ice hockey and next generations of female athletes. She and many of her teammates have decided to not play for any league in North America right now and are instead playing on teams for the PWHPA (Professional Women's Hockey Players Association). (Rosen, 2020) Knight is one of the player representatives on the board for the PWHPA, which aims to create a sustainable league for professional women's ice hockey not just for today's players, but also for the next generations to come. (PWHPA, 2021)

Hilary's journey to becoming a star both on and off the ice continues to inspire many girls and women around the globe.

She shared with me that she wants young athletes to always remember that we play sports and compete to have fun: "There are obstacles in everyday life, some harder than others, but if you really love what you do, believe in that and continue to pursue that passion, but never lose sight that sports are supposed to be fun."

PART III

PROGRESS AND THE FUTURE

FEMALE COACHES IN PROFESSIONAL SPORTS

Women coaches matter. Having played sports for almost all my life, it has always been important for me to be able to look up to female coaches in sports. A report from April 2019 from the Women's Sports Foundation found that "girls more readily identify with and see a female coach as a mentor and as a role model, which, in turn, can help counter stereotypes and boost girls' confidence, self-efficacy, and sense of belonging."

Dr. Nicole M. LaVoi is the director of the Tucker Center for Research on Girls & Women in Sport and author of the book *Women in Sports Coaching.* (University of Minnesota, 2021) She mentioned that women coaches "challenge stereotypes about gender and leadership and offer diverse perspectives, insight and advice to their athletes." (Haigh) A piece published on BSN Sports Blog in 2020 highlighted the significance of female coaches in professional sports and shared that these women are given an incredible opportunity to lead their teams and be noticed by people from around the globe.

It has been truly inspiring for young girls to see women taking on coaching roles in professional sports leagues. Back in 2012, an article that was published in *Slate* stated that there were zero female coaches for the total 122 teams in the National Basketball Association (NBA), Major League Baseball (MLB), National Hockey League (NHL), and National Football League (NFL). The article further explained, "The average NFL team employs eighteen coaches. Major League Baseball teams have six coaches and a manager. Most NHL teams carry at least four coaches, and a typical NBA squad has one head coach and four to six assistants. Altogether, that's more than one thousand jobs . . . all held by men."

However, a lot has changed since then, and women have advanced their careers as coaches in both men's and women's professional sports leagues. So many barriers have been broken down by many women, including Becky Hammon, Katie Sowers, and Bianca Smith, who have taken on incredible coaching roles in various sports.

Coach Becky Hammon is a retired WNBA player, Olympic medalist, and six-time WNBA All-Star. Outside of her incredible career as a professional athlete, she has made many strides as assistant coach of the San Antonio Spurs, an NBA team. Hammon was hired in 2014 and made history as the first female to be a full-time assistant coach in any of the four major professional men's sports leagues, which are the NBA, MLB, NHL, and NFL. A year later, she was a head coach for the San Antonio Spurs Summer League Team, and the team won the championship. (Becky Hammon, 2021)

Most recently, Becky became the first female head coach of an NBA team. The coach of San Antonio, Gregg Popovich, was ejected during the game and quickly handed the role over to Becky, saying, "You got 'em." Watching Coach Hammon call out plays and lead the Spurs team on the court was definitely a special moment for many young girls and women. It was so memorable for me because I have been watching NBA games ever since I started playing basketball in fourth grade. During the postgame interview, Becky mentioned that the history making experience was "a substantial moment." (Chappell, 2020)

Another incredible woman who has been the first to achieve a coaching milestone in her sport is Katie Sowers. Katie was hired by the San Francisco 49ers, an NFL team, as an offensive assistant coach. From a young age, she has been passionate about football and has always loved the sport: "Sowers has always known she wanted to be a coach but didn't realize it was even possible for her to do it in football. She knew football as a 'man's game' for a long time." Katie also excels as a professional athlete. She played in the Women's Football Alliance and on the United States Women's National Football Team before coaching in the NFL. (Brady, 2020)

Coach Sowers made the Super Bowl LIV truly historic. The 2020 NFL Super Bowl was so remarkable because, in addition to cheering on my hometown team, the 49ers, and watching the game with my family and friends, I saw Katie Sowers on television become the first-ever woman to coach in Super Bowl history. This moment made a lasting difference and inspired many. Katie was also featured in a Microsoft Surface commercial, in which she read a journal entry she wrote when she was a young child about how she wanted to be on a real football team one day. She ended the commercial with, "All it takes is one, and then it opens the door for so many." (Microsoft - Be The One (2020) Super Bowl with Katie Sowers, 2020)

Coach Sowers mentioned in the news that one day, before the start of the game, she "had multiple families call me over and thank me for the doors I am opening for their daughters. I even met a few young girls who were so excited to see me and tell me their own story of the sports they play. It was a special moment that I will remember for a long time." (Brady, 2020)

I had the incredible opportunity to speak with Bianca Smith who, like Becky and Katie, is a coach in a professional sports league. At the age of just three years old, Bianca was introduced to sports, and specifically to baseball, by her mom. Athletics were big in her family as she, and all her siblings, grew up playing multiple sports. While in college, Smith decided that she wanted to pursue the coaching route.

Being a woman navigating her career in the sports industry, she was initially challenged with finding coaches that would give her opportunities to gain experience: "I could read as much as I want about the game. I could research, do certifications, but without the experience I wasn't really going to get anywhere. So, the biggest thing I did was just reaching out to as many coaches as I could, and then taking whatever experience they were willing to give me."

This involved going to graduate school, and when Bianca first started out, she wasn't coaching on the field. She helped out with other tasks, such as fundraising and social media, and once she built up trust with the coaches, they were a little more willing to let her help out on the field and see what she could do. Despite facing challenges, Smith stayed motivated and persevered to reach her goal of being a baseball coach.

Her parents have also supported her along this journey, as they knew that this is something she is truly passionate about doing. Coach Smith explained that she was taught by her parents "that you spend the majority of your life working. You might as well enjoy what you do." They know she loves coaching, so they continued to push her, even during times when she kind of felt like she wanted to give up, and they still help her out to this day.

In January of 2021, Bianca Smith was officially hired as a Minor League coach by the Boston Red Sox, an MLB team. This made her the first African American woman to be a professional baseball coach. Her story has inspired many people, and this was something she didn't expect when she first took the job! Smith describes it as being "a pleasant result from getting this job."

In the future, Coach Smith hopes to see more women, and women of color, taking on coaching roles in the sports industry: "I hope it gets to a point where it isn't like national news, like a woman gets this job. I hope it's just like any other coach that gets a job." She further explained that it shouldn't be a huge deal, but rather a common thing. Whoever the best person is for the job should get it, regardless of race, gender, and ethnicity.

Taking this job is so important for Bianca because she gets to do what she loves most: coaching full-time and working with players and make a living out of it. It has also been great to see how her story can inspire other women and girls. Her one piece of advice to others would be to never give up: "Take whatever opportunity comes your way and then make it your own. A lot of the jobs that I took on, I either created myself, or I took on the new job initially, and added on responsibilities based on how I thought I could help the team." She encourages others to find where they provide value, rather than doing everything that's expected of them in regard to external pressures.

"Learn your team, learn any organization that you work for, and find out where you fit best and how you can actually help them, rather than just trying to check boxes. Because teams are going to be looking for somebody who can provide value and the ones who can, teams are going to be willing to even create positions for them." A team might not even realize that they need a specific position, but you can fill that, as long as you can show it. That's how you get your start and that's how you continue to stay in an organization. "So never give up, continue to pursue opportunities, and find where you have the best fit."

All these female coaches, and many more, are true leaders and have inspired many, including me! They have been the first in accomplishing a goal, but they will not be the last!

WOMEN IN
SPORTS MEDIA

———

In 1992, the year of the twentieth anniversary of the passage of Title IX, Dr. Mary Jo Kane, who was a faculty member at the University of Minnesota for thirty-one years, was asked by a development officer if she had any good ideas to solve the issues in women's sports. She responded that in this country, we need "a research center housed in a major research university that took seriously the study of what it meant for girls and women to participate in sports." Even though participation rates of women in athletics had exploded since Title IX passed, research universities weren't doing enough to keep up. Dr. Kane's idea was presented to Dr. Dorothy Tucker, who gave $1 million to the university to launch the Tucker Center for Research on Girls and Women in Sport. Dr. Mary Jo Kane became the first director of the research center and has spent many years working in this field, recently retiring in 2020. (McGough, 2019)

Dr. Kane is best known for her research on media coverage of female athletes. In our conversation, she shared with me how she designed a study to discover how sports fans want female athletes to be represented. She studied a group of people interested in women's sports and found that these fans wanted to see women in sports highlighted and given recognition for their athletic abilities. In the past five to seven years, Dr. Kane has seen a tremendous shift in the way the media covers and how leagues promote female athletes, versus how it was when she started her research about thirty years ago: "Finally, we are starting to portray female athletes in women's sports the way we have always portrayed men's sports, which is with respect and admiration."

In the future, Dr. Kane hopes to see an increase in the coverage of women's sports and give female athletes the recognition they deserve by continuing to convince media networks and corporate sponsors to grow the game. Anyone who is passionate about advancing women's sports can also participate by attending women's sporting events, buying season tickets, purchasing merchandise, and ensuring their local sports editors know that they are very interested in women's sports!

I myself have always been inspired by leaders who are advocating for greater coverage of women's sports. One of them is LaChina Robinson, whom I had the incredible opportunity to interview! LaChina is a reporter for ESPN and a WNBA (Women's National Basketball Association) and college basketball analyst. (LaChina Robinson, 2018) She found her passion for watching all different kinds of sports as a young girl: "I found myself captivated by competition." Robinson was a cheerleader as a teenager, but it was primarily because most of her friends were too. When she was fourteen years old, she was six feet four, and although people had told her to play basketball, she had tried it in sixth grade and wasn't really interested in it. However, one day her mom learned that LaChina could get a college scholarship playing basketball, and that was the beginning of her sports career. Her mom emphasized the importance of education and how it would be incredible if LaChina could get a college scholarship, which she did.

Robinson grew to truly love the sport of basketball, as she felt empowered on the court, made new friends, and playing basketball was an overall great personal development experience for her as a young woman. As a sports analyst and reporter, LaChina's favorite part of her job is shining light on female athletes and their incredible skills: "Women only get about 4 percent of media coverage in sport. Every day I wake up trying to change that percentage and not only give women athletes and our coaches the spotlight they deserve, but also hoping to convince some other people that they should invest in covering women's sports as they do men's sports."

LaChina has had many amazing experiences while covering competitive women's sports games, and one of her most memorable has been serving on the pregame show for the WNBA finals. In 2016, when the Minnesota Lynx were facing off against the Los Angeles Sparks in the finals, Robinson was on the court during the pregame show surrounded with all the energy that filled the stadium. This WNBA finals series went down in history and LaChina got to be a part of it! I have always loved watching the WNBA on TV, and whenever the games are close, I get so excited and nervous that I feel as if I am watching the match in person! It was so inspiring to learn that Robinson appeared on the pregame show for this game between two incredible professional women's basketball teams and highly skilled female athletes to recognize them for their hard work and dedication.

Outside of her professional career in sports, LaChina spends time giving back to the community and motivating the next generation of female sports reporters. She is the co-founder of Rising Media Stars, a nonprofit organization that works "to diversify the sports broadcasting workforce." (Rising Media Stars, 2020) During her own career, Robinson oftentimes felt lonely and confused about how she could move her journey forward in sports media, something she is very passionate about. She did have mentors guiding her along the way but feels she would have benefited a lot from having other women to encourage her or help her transition into the field of broadcasting. This inspired her to start Rising Media Stars "to give young women a training ground, mentors, and resources, where they can bridge the gap and forward their careers in sports broadcasting." People have always given to her, so LaChina believes it is important for her to give back and help others live beyond their wildest dreams, just like she was able to.

As a female athlete myself, I can certainly say that having role models like LaChina Robinson motivates us to pursue our goals and join her in recognizing female athletes. Robinson shared that there has been progress in women's sports coverage, especially with social media, which allows female athletes to be their own brand: "We can get to know them in a space where I think others have realized how amazing female athletes are and have wanted to dedicate more space and media to them." We are moving the needle, for example with endorsement deals for female athletes in recent years, but there is still a long way to go. LaChina hopes to see more sponsorship deals for women's sports leagues and players, more marketing of women's sports, and increased women's sports coverage on television.

With leaders like Robinson whom we can look up to in the sports industry, I am very hopeful about the future of media coverage for women in sports. LaChina is leading the way in bringing about change and inspiring the next generation of female athlete leaders, and I encourage you to join me in following in her footsteps by tuning into women's sports, using your platform to highlight women athletes, and "sharing the word with people of how important it is to amplify women and women's sports."

In addition to young girls being able to see themselves as professional athletes, it is crucial for them to see women having leadership roles in the sports industry as reporters, coaches, and front office staff. From a young age, I've always watched my local sports teams compete, and one of my role models has been Kerith Burke, courtside reporter for the Golden State Warriors of the National Basketball Association. Burke grew up in an athletic household and found her love for sports broadcasting at her first job out of college, which was filling in for a sports director. She shared that when she initially started her career in this field, she oftentimes found herself to be the only woman in the room. However, now the narrative has changed, because even in the past ten years, there has been an increase in the number of female sports broadcasters: "I'm definitely not the only one in there. It feels normalized, which is great because women can love and play and cover sports just as well as men can."

Kerith became the courtside reporter for the Warriors in 2017 and witnessed the team's journey to becoming a dynasty by winning back-to-back championships in 2017 and 2018. Her job makes her feel grateful every day, and she shares this passion with other young women by mentoring girls and introducing them to sports broadcasting. She explained that she sees the act of "lifting up others" and "making the path easier" for other young women to follow as her duty and responsibility: "I love this [sports broadcasting] so much, and I have to acknowledge my mentors and the people who held the doors open for me."

Burke emphasized that young girls and women who also aspire to become broadcasters for professional sports teams should always remember that their path is their own: "It's really common, maybe even normal, to compare, or to desire, what other people have. But your path will be your own." A key piece of advice that Kerith received, which she implemented in her career, was that "comparison is the thief of joy." With patience, she also learned that "it's okay to have ambition, but don't let it turn toxic. It's a lot better when you see other women on this journey as comrades, not the competition." Much like many other lessons learned through sports, this concept can be applied in our everyday lives. We should share our experience and knowledge, work to motivate those around us, and most importantly, celebrate each other's accomplishments.

FAN ENGAGEMENT IN WOMEN'S SPORTS

For many years, some have falsely believed that nobody watches women's sports because they are "boring." However, many female athlete leagues have shown otherwise as their fan engagement has been on the rise. Various women's sports have made great strides, proving that many fans are interested in watching their competitive and athletic games. Also, in recent years, women's sports have received a unique type of engagement from its fans that has been very different from other sports, men's and women's, in the past.

In the past, attempts to start a female sports league have failed. Cathy Engelbert, commissioner of the Women's National Basketball Association (WNBA), shared that the league will soon be entering its twenty-fifth season, making it "the first women's sports league in the US to actually survive that long." When the COVID-19 pandemic hit in March, the WNBA was forced to change its plans. The league decided that the players would compete in a bubble in Florida, which meant that all the athletes would stay in a specific city for the duration of the season. Despite having no in-person fans for the 2020 season, the WNBA drew "an audience in historic numbers" and the league reported that there was a "68 percent increase in regular-season viewership across all networks." Engelbert shared that there are still those people who will criticize and oppose women's sports, but many are starting to stand up and say the truth—that WNBA players are very skilled at their sport and compete at a high level. (DiTrolio, 2020) I myself was very glad to hear this, because basketball was one of my earliest sports and I have looked up to many athletes in the WNBA as my role models.

Interest in women's sports has been increasing on the global level too. A 2018 research study done by The Nielsen Company, which was conducted in eight countries around the world, found that "66 percent of the population is interested in at least one women's sport" and "84 percent of general sports fans are interested in women's sports." They reported that of these sports fans, 49 percent are female and 51 percent are male, showing that women aren't the only group interested in female athletics. Fan engagement for Team USA's female athletes in recent years has also proven that many people enjoy watching women's sports. Team USA reported in 2018 that for the PyeongChang Olympic Winter Games, "the most engaging Facebook post was a photo link to the TeamUSA. org recap of the women's ice hockey team capturing gold over Canada." (Team USA, 2018)

Women's soccer has done exceptionally well in the past few years with building an authentic fan base and advocating for equality in all sports too. FIFA (Fédération Internationale de

Football Association) reported in 2019 that a record-breaking total of 1.12 billion people viewed the 2019 Women's World Cup and the final game in this competition (USA vs. Netherlands) "was the most watched FIFA Women's World Cup match ever." Although soccer is a sport I have not participated in before, I did watch this World Cup competition. I remember being so inspired by our country's top female soccer players as I watched their championship celebration and listened to their victory speeches afterward. This was also the first time when I learned more about how the game of soccer is played.

The National Women's Soccer League (NWSL), a "Division I women's professional soccer league featuring national team players from around the world," has been closely attached to working towards gender equality in sports. I spoke to Lindsay Barenz, the former vice president of Business Development at the NWSL and current president of business operations at the Washington Spirit of the NWSL, about fan engagement in women's sports and specifically in women's soccer. The league is now entering its ninth year, making it the longest surviving professional women's soccer league in the United States. It is also the third attempt at making a professional league for women's soccer in the United States, since the first two did not survive. (NWSL, 2020)

Lindsay mentioned that fans of women's soccer are unique because they are not only knowledgeable about the sport, but they also know about the business of women's soccer. They don't just engage passively, by liking and retweeting posts, but also actively in a strategic way to support the game. For example, she explained that if you search on Twitter for NWSL and Secret deodorant, you will find tweets of people saying, "I just went out and bought some Secret deodorant because they are a sponsor of the NWSL." A lot of other tweets will also come up of fans saying thank you Secret deodorant, P&G (Procter & Gamble), Google, and Verizon for being sponsors of the NWSL and supporting women's soccer. I actually tried this after talking to Lindsay and, as she mentioned, many tweets about people supporting these brands because of their partnership with the NWSL came up. She explained that "I think that's a very different type of engagement than you would see in the NFL (National Football League) or the NBA (National Basketball Association). They have many more numbers than us, but our fans are engaged in a very proactive and methodical way to try to help support the league. Our fans understand the connection between the success of our corporate partnerships and our ability to sustain a week."

Another way that women's soccer fans engage in a unique way is by holding people accountable. Lindsay gave an example of an event that occurred this past year. The NWSL was the first professional team sport to return to play during the pandemic in the United States. Even though they did get attention for this, they were also overlooked by a lot of sports writers who would talk about the return to play and highlight men's leagues, without acknowledging that the first league to return to play was actually the NWSL. These comments did not go unchecked by the NWSL's fan base; the sports writers got a lot of feedback and pushback when they made inaccurate statements. Barenz mentioned that this kind of forceful, in unison, holding people accountable on the internet on behalf of women's sports and the NWSL is unique.

When I asked Lindsay what makes fans so personally connected to women's soccer, she said that it has to do with the roots of women's sports in the United States. Women have been vilified for being athletes and told they don't belong because playing sports does not comport with their gender norms. However, despite all this "criticism and pressure against being athletes, women in the United States continue to pursue athletics." Specifically, the US Women's National Soccer Team has been dominant globally in their sport, having won multiple World Cup titles and Olympics medals. Therefore, people are fans of women's soccer because they're fans of the sport and the women athletes in the US who are very skilled at it. Barenz says that what makes them unique is that "they also view themselves as champions of a cause and wanting to demand respect and to celebrate these incredible world-class athletes." This passion for activism and advocacy is almost always intertwined with being a fan of women's soccer.

The driving force behind the success of the NWSL, the third attempt at making a professional women's soccer league in the United States, has been sponsorship. Lindsay explained that the league makes revenue from ticket sales, broadcast deals, and from their sponsors. Historically, women's sports have lagged behind their male counterparts in all three of these areas but especially so in corporate sponsorship. We are seeing change in this area for two key reasons. First of all, brands are realizing that in reality, it is actually a good investment to sponsor women's leagues because their audience is sizable enough, ensuring that the company gets an automatic return on their investment from day one. The other reason is that when brands partner with the NWSL or other women's sports leagues, they send "a loud and clear message" to their customers, future customers, and employees that they support women and believe in equal opportunity for both women and girls, and men and boys, to pursue their dreams. These companies also send a message to their audience that they believe women should be paid their worth.

Barenz shared, "Based on research that the NWSL has done, when a company sponsors the NWSL, our fans believe that the company supports gender equality . . . or they support diversity, equality, and inclusion initiatives. We have evidence that when a brand signs on to the NWSL, they get that halo effect of being known for the fact that they support women." This adds real value to a company because we're living in 2021 when every brand wants to be known for supporting women. Also, Lindsay mentioned that there are very few ways for brands to authentically communicate this message: "You can stand up on stage and support women, which is probably a good thing to do, and it's certainly wise to say that and not the opposite, but how do you actually demonstrate a commitment to women? There are very few ways to authentically do that, but one way is to be a corporate partner of the NWSL."

With all this recent success, Barenz believes that "we are just now beginning to realize the potential for growing the audience of women's soccer." In the lifetime of the NWSL, they have had many broadcasting arrangements but rarely ever got many corporate partnerships; however, this greatly changed in 2019. "On the tail of the 2019 Women's World Cup, we believed it was a tipping point, and in retrospect, I think that is exactly right." The NWSL hired an agency specializing in sports broadcasting rights who went out and did a thorough process in which they talked to many channels, not making any assumptions about who would or wouldn't be interested in the league's broadcast rights.

This was a huge success as the NWSL got multiyear deals with CBS (the largest broadcast network in the country) and Twitch (one of the most innovative streaming platforms in the world) and got a multiyear sponsorship with Verizon. Lindsay shared that even during the COVID-19 pandemic, the league was able to put on a tournament called the Challenge Cup, in which both Secret deodorant and Google were corporate partners: "We did not know what to expect when we put our games on CBS. . . . We quadrupled our audience instantly." This also serves as a perfect example that people do want to watch women's sports and that making women's sports games easily accessible to fans makes a huge difference: "Once you put it in front of them and you market it to them and you say it's very easy, it shows here on CBS All Access or CBS or Twitch, people show up, and they enjoy themselves and they come back." In 2020, the NWSL did not know for certain whether the fans would return or if this type of viewership was sustainable. They thought it might have been a miracle or maybe many people viewed the games because there were no other live sports on TV since the league was the first to return to play in the US. However, later in the year, the league put on more games, "and again, hundreds of thousands of people showed up. That's many more people than used to watch our games when we had them on other outlets."

The United States Women's National Soccer Team's (USWNT) incredible performance in the World Cup and the growth of the NWSL in recent years has not only impacted women's soccer, but it has also had a broader influence on all female sports as a whole. Lindsay shared that when a person sees women as athletes, it breaks apart the stereotypes regarding gender in sports and athletics. She gave an example of if someone becomes a fan of Alex Morgan, a soccer star on the USWNT, "then the next time they see a WNBA player, or a woman lacrosse player, or a woman hockey player," there won't be a conflict with their view of what a woman can be: "I think anytime any woman succeeds in sports, whether that's track and field [athletes] or swimmers at the Olympics, it benefits all women in all sports."

WORKING TOGETHER TO ADVANCE WOMEN'S SPORTS

———

Three-time NBA Champion. Two-time NBA Most Valuable Player. Seven-time NBA All-Star. (Low, 2021) Stephen Curry is not only known for his success as a basketball player, but also as a star off the court. He has been using his platform in several ways to encourage female youth participation in sports. His commitment to this cause has proven that by collectively working to create gender equality in sports, we can achieve real change. I have been watching the National Basketball Association (NBA) since I was in elementary school and ever since then, I have bought many of Steph's jerseys and have his poster hanging up in my room. He has been my favorite NBA player not just for his incredible skills as a professional athlete, but also because he sends a powerful message to so many young athletes in sports through his advocacy and initiatives.

Back in 2018, Curry launched his first annual free all-girls basketball camp in the San Francisco Bay Area: "We want to be able to instill the confidence in girls that they can be a part of the game as well and do special things with the game." (NBA, 2018) Shortly after, on Women's Equality Day (August 26, 2018), he published an article on The Players' Tribune in which he shared a thoughtful and touching message about gender equality. In his article, "This is Personal," he shared how his passion for creating equal opportunities in sports stemmed from his own story. Referring to his mom and wife as being "incredible and fiercely principled" women, he explained that because of them, he has been educated on the topic of women's equality. One of the most important things he has learned through his own life has been: "to always stay listening to women, to always stay believing in women, and—when it comes to anyone's expectations for women—to always stay challenging the idea of what's right." (Curry, 2018)

Steph is also the father of two young daughters, which makes the topic of gender equality even more personal to him. He mentioned in his article that he wants his daughters to grow up knowing that their gender does not hold them back. Another important topic Curry touched on in his article was equal pay; he also encouraged his readers to work collectively to achieve this goal. He pointed out that people should not only advocate for equal pay on Women's Equality Day, but rather everyday: "Every day—that's when we need to be working to close the pay gap in this country. Because every day is when the pay gap is affecting women. And every day is when the pay gap is sending the wrong message to women about who they are, and how they're valued, and what they can or cannot become." (Curry, 2018)

In this article, Curry also shared his recent experience of hosting his first all-girls basketball camp and the message he hoped to convey to others. In addition to teaching that basketball, and sports in general, are not only for boys, Steph also had another goal in mind: "It's just basketball. Played by women and celebrated by everyone." This camp was just the beginning of Stephen's role as an advocate for women's sports, as he stated in his article that he is "feeling more driven than ever." (Curry, 2018)

His drive to make change in this field was evident as he continued to launch new initiatives to work toward gender equality in sports. In November of 2018, nine-year-old Riley Morrison wrote a letter to Curry telling him that she is a big fan of his and knows he supports female athletes, but when she was buying new shoes for her upcoming basketball season, she was disappointed to discover the Curry 5 was only sold in the boy's section. Steph responded to Morrison's letter, thanking her for bringing up the issue. He fixed the problem right away and even told Riley that he would personally send her a pair of Curry 5 shoes. Riley's letter was not only written to address her own concern but also as a way to speak up for other young girls in sports. Once again, Curry sent a powerful message to his fans that basketball is a game for everyone. (Buxeda, 2018)

The impact that Riley and Steph made on girls and women's sports did not end in November. The following year, during Women's History Month (March), the NBA superstar launched the Curry 6 "United We Win" shoes on International Women's Day (March 8). He chose Riley to design the sock liner for this shoe; she drew pictures of girls playing basketball on it and wrote inspiring messages, like "Play With Heart" and "Be the Change." Riley came to Curry's store for the launch of this new shoe she had helped design to give some interviews—to her surprise, she also got the chance to meet Steph! (Anderson, 2019) A 2019 article by Joel Anderson of ESPN reported this was "believed to be the first time a marquee male athlete has been the face of a basketball shoe made specifically for women and girls."

Continuing his advocacy for gender equality, Curry worked with the Eat. Learn. Play. Foundation, a nonprofit he co-founded with his wife, Ayesha, to award college scholarships to deserving young girls. He invited the recipients of this scholarship to come to the Golden State Warriors game on International Women's Day. Stephen and Ayesha Curry's Eat. Learn. Play. Foundation also partnered with Chase Bank to start It's Our Game, a ticket platform that spotlights "local organizations that are making a difference in girls' lives and surprising them with Warriors tickets to celebrate all of the great work they're doing for the community." (@stephencurry30, October 11, 2019) They kicked off this initiative by inviting seven girls from Oakland High School to attend the first Golden State Warriors game at the newly built Chase Center. (Rodriguez, 2019)

Curry's advocacy and encouragement of girls and women in sports continues to make a lasting impact. He made his all-girls basketball camp an annual event and in 2019, he also invited women leaders in sports to share their inspiring journeys with the campers. He shared that "the purpose of the event is to allow the girls a chance to learn how to be successful 'not just in the world of sports, but beyond—anything that you put your mind to.'" (NBA, 2019)

The NBA star made another shoe dedicated to girls and women for International Women's Day 2020. (Under Armour, Inc., 2020) He partnered with actress and advocate Storm Reid, who uses her platform to inspire girls through her Bamazing initiative. Storm's initiative "aims to empower young girls by helping them discover and nurture their inner light through the encouragement of positive declarations of self" and their "goal is to put emphasis on the uplifting qualities within each of us that will lead to more self-love and empathy for others." (@stormreid, September 1, 2018)

Steph and Storm collaborated to launch the Curry 7 Bamazing colorway shoe. Similar to the shoe designed by Riley Morrison, this one had powerful messages written on its sock liner, like "Bbrave" and "Btrue." (Under Armour, Inc., 2020) These messages paralleled Bamazing's principle that "promoting a healthy self-esteem early on, will give the youth a head-start in molding a healthier and more tolerant future. Everything is possible when you are confident about all the things you can be." (@stormreid, September 1, 2018)

By using his platform to empower young girls and women in sports, Stephen Curry has not only made a difference in the lives of female athletes, like myself, but has also shown that everyone can play an important and powerful role in this movement too. By launching several initiatives, advocating for gender equality, and creating opportunities for young girls to play the beautiful game of basketball, Curry has shown that by working together, we will achieve significant change in the field of women's sports.

KEEPING GIRLS
IN THE GAME

———

The Teen Sport Report, published by the Women's Sports Foundation in 2018, found that "40 percent of teen girls are not actively participating in sport." Almost half of teenage girls aren't playing sports for several reasons, including social stigmas, not having positive role models to look up to, and a lack of access—in fact, the Women's Sports Foundation shared that "girls have 1.3 million fewer opportunities to play high school sports than boys have."

Having played sports all my life, and continuing to do so now, I have felt the benefits that participating in athletics has on all children, including learning to work in a team and becoming confident in oneself. This has inspired me to work to make the future of sports better for the next generations of girls. I have also had the incredible opportunity to speak and learn from three amazing organizations that are also on a mission to keep girls in the game, making me even more hopeful for the future.

When I discovered the Women's Sports Foundation last year, I knew right away that its values aligned with mine. I also attended its virtual event this year for National Girls and Women in Sports Day and was absolutely blown away by all the inspiring female athlete leaders and the work they're doing to achieve gender equality in sports. Even through a computer screen, the athletes' passion to create a better future for women's sports was evident, and they were able to connect with all the young girls who were watching the event that day.

The nonprofit organization was founded by tennis legend Billie Jean King in 1974 and since then has been working to build "a future where every girl and woman can play, be active, and realize her full potential." The organization is not only based on community impac, but also incorporates research, partnerships, and advocacy "to transform the game so that every girl and woman can realize her power." (Women's Sports Foundation, 2021)

Phaidra Knight, a former professional rugby player and current president of the Women's Sports Foundation, spoke with me about the importance of using her platform as a female athlete to give back and advocate. She has always loved athletics as she started playing sports at the age of three. While at law school, Knight discovered rugby. She shared that one of her most memorable experiences was winning her first national championship with her club team, whom she had trained and practiced diligently with. Phaidra also went on to play rugby at the international level in 1999 with Team USA and was inducted into the World Rugby Hall of Fame in 2017.

Outside of her professional athletic career, she dedicates time to advancing girls and women's sports too. When I spoke with

Phaidra, she mentioned, "There are so many people who need amplification of their voices. If I'm in a position and have a platform to do that, I feel like it's my duty to help bring more exposure, resources, and attention to the causes that I believe in and support." Knight has been serving the community with the Women's Sports Foundation for over twenty-three years, starting as an advocacy intern, then becoming an athlete ambassador, and now being the president and serving on the board of trustees. Being involved with the organization for so long, Phaidra is excited "to be in this role and see all of the incredible changes and differences that this organization has made in so many lives of girls and women across the country." She encourages other girls and advocates for gender equality in sports to continue the fight for equity.

As a female athlete and advocate for women's sports myself, I try my best to advance the work that is being done to level the playing field. As a part of this journey, I recently joined the Voice in Sport High School Advocacy Leadership Team. Voice in Sport (VIS) was founded in 2019 by Stef Strack, a sports industry executive who previously worked at Nike and was the CEO of Rag & Bone. Stef left her career in the footwear and apparel industry to pursue her true passion of advocating for women's sports by creating Voice in Sport—another incredible example of women empowering women! The mission of VIS is to "bring more visibility to girls and women in sport and elevate their voice." In addition to advocating for girls and women in sport, Voice in Sport is creating specific content for them fueled by a team of women athlete content contributors called VIS Creators. (VIS Holdings Inc, 2021)

VIS provides a platform and a safe community for young girls to access mentorship from college and professional women athletes and group or one-on-one sessions with the top experts in sport psychology, sports nutrition, and women's health. (VIS Holdings Inc, 2021) I was fortunate to speak with Taylor Cummings, who is considered to be the best female collegiate lacrosse player in the country. She is also a part of the VIS League, dedicating time to mentoring and supporting young girls and women in sports.

When Taylor was five years old, she moved from Richmond to Maryland, where lacrosse is the "state sport." She saw all of her friends playing lacrosse and decided to try it out since she'd always been active and enjoys playing sports. Throughout high school, Taylor also participated in soccer and basketball but ended up pursuing lacrosse in college at the University of Maryland. Cummings had an incredible collegiate career, making the national championship all four years and winning two times. Since 2013, she has been on the United States Women's National Lacrosse Team and has competed in the World Games and the World Cup, which take place in various countries around the globe. She mentioned that some of her most memorable experiences playing lacrosse on the US team have been "continuing to meet such amazing women who love the game and are great people and really want to just see it flourish."

I asked Cummings, who is a VIS League mentor for young women athletes, why her role in the VIS community is so important to her. She explained that when she was in high school, she would have loved to have someone to talk to who has been in her shoes. She also said that she found her home in athletics because lacrosse has taught her so many life lessons, including learning how to be on a team, communicating, and owning her confidence. One thing that Taylor shared that truly stood out to me was that "We are role models and are working with the next generation to make sure that you have it better than we had it, in terms of our treatment or the leagues we're in—more so just to make sure you have someone to lean on if you're going through a tough time."

Taylor is also passionate about coaching as she holds lacrosse clinics across the country and also coaches at the high school she played at, McDonogh School. In addition to mentoring young girls, Cummings loves the idea that she can teach them a lot of life lessons through a sport they all share a passion for. She was fortunate to have incredible coaches herself who love women's sports and tries to follow their footsteps to be the coach that she remembers them being for herself and her teammates.

One of her main goals as a coach is to "provide an environment where our players can grow." She wants them to learn to take risks and try to make a mistake, knowing that they have a safe space to come back to and try again. Taylor shared that her coach at Maryland said it best, which was that "you won't remember scores, you won't remember how you played in a game, but you'll remember the people that you were with, the relationships you made, the experiences you had, and that's what is going to be the most important at the end of the day."

The one piece of advice she would give to athletes and women in sports would be to chase after whatever dreams you have, because there is no one who can stand in your way except yourself. She also wants to emphasize that we should have fun while playing sports, rather than putting pressure on ourselves to be perfect all the time: "Get to the next thing and try to just be where your feet are and have fun and enjoy who you're with because at the end of the day that's who matters." I was not only amazed by Cummings' amazing athletic career, but her passion to coach and mentor young female athletes truly touched my heart. I strongly believe that role models like Taylor and communities like Voice in Sport have the power to change, and currently are changing, the field of women's sports for the better and inspiring young girls to participate in sports.

Since basketball is the sport I've been playing the longest, and I've been watching the NBA (National Basketball Association) and WNBA (Women's National Basketball Association) since I started playing, I was so excited when I found out that the NBA, WNBA, and Jr. NBA launched Her Time to Play. This is "a national initiative that is dedicated to championing change on behalf of girls and women and providing them with ways to connect, collaborate, and actively engage with one another through the game of basketball." (Jr. NBA, 2021) I loved learning more about Her Time to Play in my conversation with Nicole Breen and Candice Haynes, who manage this incredible initiative. Nicole shared that in 2017, statistics were published that shared that basketball was no longer the top team sport for girls in high school, and by age fourteen, girls were also dropping out of sports two times the rate of boys. She and her colleagues realized that if they wanted to help change the participation trends, they needed to be more intentional about offering programs that are specific to girls, rather than co-ed, which led to the idea of launching a girls participation initiative.

I love the empowering message that comes from the initiative's name, Her Time to Play, and Nicole mentioned, "We want girls to be active and to have fun. As much as we want to develop basketball players and NBA and WNBA fans, we really want girls in general to learn the values you gain from playing any sport and to have a positive experience where they leave feeling good about themselves." To launch the initiative, they partnered with the Women's Sports Foundation, which does a lot of research about girls and women's sports, to co-create a girls-specific basketball-focused curriculum that incorporates social emotional learning. It also includes personal stories from WNBA players about how they faced similar challenges young girls and women in sports face today and how it impacted them in their life.

As a young female athlete myself, I know that hearing the stories of our role models inspires us to keep playing sports. Her Time to Play also focuses on organizing a variety of events for girls, including basketball clinics, panel discussions, leadership summits, and more. Numerous WNBA and NBA players even joined one of their biggest all-girls clinics during the 2020 All Star in Chicago! Additionally, Her Time to Play works to support coaches on how to coach girls' sports teams, as we know that having positive coaches, particularly for girls, truly makes all the difference in empowering young athletes. I felt so motivated when I heard about this, because I've seen and felt the impact that coaches have on their players. The initiative also encourages organizations to incorporate female coaches and mentors into their programming because they "have a significant impact on girls' participation that goes beyond the court." (Jr NBA, 2021)

Candice also emphasized that they view the program as being more than just basketball: "We really want to use Her Time to Play to create a community around girls' basketball, girls' wellness and physical activity and just overall girls' empowerment and development." The initiative has already made an impact in encouraging more girls to participate in not only Her Time to Play events but also the Jr. NBA's co-ed events. Nicole and Candice shared that before Her Time to play started, most of the Jr. NBA's co-ed programs were heavily male. They've seen that by associating a specific brand to girls, it made them feel more comfortable and confident in general to come out to play basketball with their friends.

In the future, Candice and Nicole hope to continue growing the Her Time to Play community by expanding their curriculum, developing more resources to share directly with girls and their parents, and continuing to provide educational and developmental opportunities to coaches working with girls, because mentorship is truly important to keep girls in the game. From personal experience, I have learned that sports provide a lot of value, so we must work to ensure that all children are given the opportunity to play sports and stay active. Especially when I look at the work that all these organizations are doing, I feel empowered to carry this mission forward.

YOUNG GIRLS
MAKING CHANGE

———

I have always believed in the idea of the younger generation having the responsibility to carry the torch forward and lead the change that we see our leaders and role models taking part in. This not only inspired me to write a book about women's sports but also gave me the incredible opportunity to meet other young girls who are passionate about making change in this field, whether that be regarding equal pay, more opportunities for young girls to participate in sports, or increased media coverage for women's sports. Age truly is just a number, as girls who are just six years old are also driving the change in girls and women's sports!

When I spoke to Professor Marie Hardin from Penn State University, she also shared the idea of continuing to push for change for female athletes. She explained that by taking the long view when looking at the advancement of women's sports over time, it is evident that there has been progress and gradual change, as conditions weren't the same twenty years ago: "This is not a light switch, this is a dimmer. It's not an on or off light switch. This is like a dimmer that's going to turn very, very slowly." Our goal is to create a positive culture around women's sports, give female athletes the recognition they deserve, and work to ensure that girls are encouraged to and given the opportunity to participate in a variety of sports from a young age. All the change won't happen tomorrow, but it will add up and make a significant impact over time.

Many young girls are driving change in women's sports. I had the incredible opportunity to interview two inspiring young advocates: Samantha Gordon, a high school senior from Utah, and Pepper Persley, a ten-year-old WNBA reporter.

Sam shared with me that she had always been playing football outside with her brothers or during recess with the boys. She started playing on a team when she was just nine years old after watching her older brother play competitive football. Sam used to go with her dad to pick up her brother from football practice and since the players would run wind sprints at the end, she used to ask her dad if she could join them. She beat most of the boys on the team, even though they were three years older than her, and soon it became routine that Sam would run wind sprints with her brother and his teammates. She mentioned, "After a while, the coach made a competition out of it, like, 'Beat Gordon's sister!' After one of the practices, he [the coach] told me that I should try playing football and he thinks that I'd be really good at it."

This prompted Sam to train hard for three months leading up to the tryouts. She never knew how big of a deal this would be; she was just a young girl going out and playing the sport she loved, football. During tryouts, Sam scored first out of 172 boys in almost every speed and agility drill. Although she never really noticed the fact that she was the only girl playing football with a group of boys, there were definitely moments during tryouts that made her feel targeted. Some boys would start chants in line to "beat the girl," and parents would come onto the field and yell at their son to not get beat by a girl when Sam would tackle them. However, once Sam got onto her actual team, she had an amazing first season of football, an awesome coach, and absolutely dominated the tackle football league!

Her love for the game of football, along with the support of her dad and brother, outweighed all the negative comments she heard on the field: "Instead of letting it really affect me, I focused on just going out and deciding to prove them wrong, because there's nothing better than scoring a touchdown on a boy who didn't think girls can play football." Sam's father made a video of her football highlights, which included scoring twenty-five touchdowns, having sixty-five tackles, and running for 1,911 yards in one season! It went viral on the internet, getting almost five million views in just three days! She had many incredible experiences that followed, such as being featured on a Wheaties cereal box, meeting superstar athletes, including NFL (National Football League) and US Women's National Soccer Team players, and being a part of NFL commercials. (Gordon and Bruening, 2013)

Gordon uses her platform to advocate and create opportunities for all girls and women to play football. In addition to publishing *Sweet Feet: Sam Gordon's Winning Season*, a book that shares her story, Sam started the Utah Girls Tackle

Football League. She mentioned that the league started out with fifty girls in its first year and now has about five hundred girls! (UTGFL, 2019) Sam explained that just like the jump in the number of girls playing high school sports after Title IX passed, the league shows that it's not that girls don't want to participate in sports or play football, but rather they aren't always given the opportunity to: "I honestly was kind of expecting a lot of girls to come out because I had so many who told me that they wanted to play."

It has been incredible to see how the league has continued to grow over the years and the number of girls that come out to play, from elementary ages to high school. Sam has especially loved seeing other girls falling in love with the sport. My high school only offers an annual flag football game for girls to participate in, but I know that I would definitely play in a tackle football league if one was offered, as I have always loved playing and watching football with my brother and friends.

Sam also shared with me the broader impact of football and sports in general: "I think football is a sport unlike any other. It's the most popular sport in America, the thing that is fantasized in high school and the football boys are like worshiped, and the Super Bowl is like the most watched sporting event in the world. Football dominates everything and girls have almost no part in it." There has been a lot of progress in the field of girls and women's sports, but football is something that still needs to be conquered; it's like one of the final barriers to achieving equal play. Sam also believes that playing sports is important for every girl because it creates leadership opportunities and helps to make new friends by playing with teammates.

In the future, Sam hopes to make girls' football a sanctioned high school sport. She is currently working on a Title IX lawsuit against a few school districts and hopes this will force high schools to offer a separate girls' tackle football team. If it doesn't work in this case, Sam will continue to work towards this goal: "It might take a very long time because there is a stigma around it, but I think girls' tackle football has unlimited potential." I absolutely agree with this and was so amazed by the impact Sam has had on girls not just in her community but across the nation. She was recently given the NFL Game Changer Award and I was so inspired when I heard her award speech. One line that touched me was: "Before Title IX, some people thought that girls were not interested in playing sports. But they were wrong. They were just as wrong as people who argued that women did not want to vote, to hold public office, or to be lawyers or doctors. People who think girls don't want to play football are wrong too." (NFL Honors Utah Girls Tackle Football with Game Changer Award, 2018)

When I asked Sam about how she feels about making an impact on so many young girls and women like myself, she mentioned that it's crazy to think about, because as a little nine-year old going out to play football against the boys, she didn't think much of it. She loves the idea that she can help a girl, as one of her favorite things to do is attending Saturday elementary-aged football games for the Utah Girls Tackle Football League. Sam enjoys watching the girls play and seeing their excited faces when she talks to them after the game. It is especially incredible for her to see the younger generation, how she can have an impact on them, and change the world.

One of her most memorable experiences as a football star and advocate for girls and women's sports has been playing during halftime during the NFL Pro Bowl. She shared that the NFL has been so supportive and gave twenty-two girls from her league an amazing opportunity to train for three weeks before the Pro Bowl and then play during halftime. Sam mentioned, "It was incredible because it was an actual NFL stadium. The crowds were huge, everybody was cheering, and it felt like a real game. Everybody played great and I think we went out and showed that girls can play football too to a lot of people." Afterward, Sam and her teammates walked around the stadium while wearing their jerseys as fans congratulated them. Sam will never forget the experience that her team had to play on a real field in front of a big crowd and showcase their abilities as female football players. Sam Gordon ended her speech when receiving the NFL Game Changer Award with five powerful words: "Equality is our Super Bowl." (NFL Honors Utah Girls Tackle Football with Game Changer Award, 2018)

Another young girl who is making change in girls' and women's sports is Pepper Persley. Pepper, a ten-year-old WNBA journalist, proved that age is just a number. Her genuine curiosity led her to her first interview with WNBA player Sugar Rodgers when she was just six years old! This was a special moment, but Pepper's career truly started when she was seven. I asked Pepper what inspired her to become a journalist and start her own show and podcast at such a young age; her response was so incredible!

"I wanted to bring more attention to the WNBA, so I conducted a series of interviews hoping to show people how awesome the WNBA was. Then, during quarantine this year, I wanted to bring a smile to people's faces, so I started *Dish With Pepper*, my Instagram Live talk show and podcast, because I knew it was tough being stuck at home."

For her show and podcast, *Dish With Pepper*, she has interviewed many amazing people, including basketball Hall of Famer Katie Smith, activist and mayoral candidate for New York City Maya Wiley, and author and journalist Liz Plank. Pepper mentioned that she has had a lot of awesome experiences while doing her job and highlighted some of her most memorable ones.

She has been involved with the Women's Sports Foundation (WSF), presenting the Wilma Rudolph Courage Award to the WNBA and interviewing WNBA player Layshia Clarendon during the WSFs 2020 Salute to Women in Sports. Pepper also co-hosted the Women's Sports Foundation's 2021 National Girls and Women in Sports Day Girls Fest. I watched this event live on the WSF YouTube Channel and was so inspired by Pepper!

Throughout the 2020 WNBA season, Pepper attended conferences for most of the WNBA teams. She also asked questions during the Seattle Storm's 2020 WNBA championship press conference! Some of the WNBA stars she has interviewed include Breanna Stewart of the Seattle Storm, Renee Montgomery, former WNBA player and current co-owner of the Atlanta Dream, and Natasha Cloud of the Washington Mystics. Pepper has been both the interviewer and the interviewee; she shared with me how she has been featured on news channels too!

Pepper was interviewed on CBS Sports Network by basketball analyst Debbie Antonelli during the broadcast of a WNBA game. She was also featured on an episode of *Top of HER Game* with her "big sis" and mentor, Meghan McPeak, who is a basketball broadcaster. I asked Pepper about the change she hopes to see in the future of women's sports. She responded that more sports networks need to recognize the impact of women's sports. Pepper shared the truth in her response regarding the message the sports media sends to young girls.

"They [sports networks] also need to understand that there will always be little girls and kids who watch their networks and don't see women. We need more women's sports coverage. Because, first and foremost, they are amazing athletes. Secondly, they use their platforms to bring about change all the time. For me, it is amazing to be able to see the women of the WNBA play incredible basketball and hear their message, but not enough kids know of the WNBA and so many other professional women's sports leagues."

The ten-year-old journalist also explained that female athletes have repeatedly proved that they are worthy of coverage, so people who work in sports media need to become more knowledgeable about the importance of women's sports. In addition, "People who already cover women's sports need to promote it as well. In terms of TV coverage, I just think more popular news sources need to step up and talk about both men's and women's sports."

At the young age of ten, Pepper has already made a huge impact on women's sports by giving female athletes the recognition they deserve on her podcast and talk show. She has also inspired many young girls and athletes, including myself! Her one piece of advice is: "Believe in yourself no matter what people do to try and stop you. If you work hard toward something then, you can absolutely achieve it!"

Professor Hardin mentioned that she encourages everyone, including young girls, to continue advocating because everyone's work is truly important: "You need to think about this as building a house, one brick at a time; every brick, you've got to have every brick. So every voice, every person who advocates, every person who consumes [women's sports], everybody matters, ultimately. So put your brick, put your brick up in the wall. We need it." I am working to put my brick up in the wall and I encourage you to do the same, so that we can all build this house together!

All the experiences that female athletes have had in recent years are connected and shared with stories of women from the past. Whether it be in education, politics, sports, or the workplace, women have had it the hard way for years. We have made significant progress toward gender equality, thanks to both women and men advocating for change and are hopeful that the challenges girls and women face today won't last forever. Serena Williams, legendary tennis player and equal rights advocate, says it best: "We must continue to dream big, and in doing so, we empower the next generation of women to be just as bold in their pursuits." (Williams, 2016)

ACKNOWLEDGMENTS

—

Thank you to Almighty Waheguru Ji for giving me the strength to write this book.

I would also like to thank my mom, dad, brother Mantej, and extended family for always believing in me and encouraging me to chase after my dreams. I am truly grateful for your love and support.

A special thanks to all the athletes, researchers, advocates, leaders, and professionals in women's sports who took time out of their busy schedules to share their inspiring stories and valuable insights with me. This book would not be possible without you:

Alana Nichols, Lindsey Vonn, Kendall Coyne Schofield, Lauren Fisher, Kristi Yamaguchi, Melissa Stockwell, Marie Hardin, Diane McClelland, Suzanne Lackman, Brandi Chastain, Kathrine Switzer, Renee Montgomery, Lindsay Barenz, Ellen J. Staurowsky, Phaidra Knight, LaChina Robinson, Meghan Duggan, Hilary Knight, Sam Gordon, Pepper Persley, Mary Jo Kane, Nicole Breen, Candice Haynes, Taylor Cummings, Stef Strack, Bianca Smith, Dana Weintraub, Kerith Burke, and Rhea Wadia.

I'd like to recognize everyone from the *She Plays to Win* author community who supported my prelaunch campaign and made the publishing of this book possible. Thank you for rooting for me!

Jaspreet Kaur, Eric Koester, Dana Weintraub, Ravinder Singh, Michael Lasevich, Max Espaillat, Manoj Kunjappan, Michael Carrow, Michele Yamaguchi, Vedika Jawa, Harnoor Kaur, Desmond Dunham, Aaron Yu, Prabhu Inbarajan, Lanea Tuiasosopo, Upneet Singh, Chloe Muela, Caroline Heldman, Kate Edwards, Lily Mei, Angelina M Dayton, Sherri Shaner, Deepak Sharma, Rachel Bernstein, Nathan Candaner, Simar Kaur, Mantej Singh, Michael Senadenos, Bandagi Kaur, Satinder Chhatwal, Tim Hovis, Taranjit Singh, Umang Gopani, Radakrishna V, Reena Johl, Chloe Dang, Harpreet Everest, Rashminder Khangura-Taggar, Kerith Burke, Jasleen Kaur & Tarunpreet Singh, Taranjit Singh Lamba, Harneel & Aneet Mangat, Jasdeep Singh, Suzanne Kinner, Bryan Gebhardt, Mangal Singh, Caroline Mattise, Nimrit Kaur, Iasmine Abdennabi, Mandeep Kaur, Arzu Ozbek, Ekam & Anandleen Kaur, Harminder Jagpal, James Ray, Judith Denery, Gita Asuti, Deborah Todd, Navjeet Singh, Colleen McFarland, Tanroop Kaur, Sneha Kaur, Gurmeet S Kalra, Manat Kaur, Ashmit Bhattacharya, Manvir Singh, Nirvair Singh, Sukhwinder Singh, Nicole Norman, Harmeet Singh, Teresa Singh, Jagat Singh Khalsa, Kaanthi Pandhigunta, Gurleen Kaur, Tejleen Kaur, Japneet Kaur, Keerat Kaur, Yi Cui, Maria DeGuzman, Linda Haastrup, and Chelsea Zhang.

A huge thanks to my amazing editors, Erika Arroyo and Judy Rosen, for all their hard work and dedication. Thank you for not only providing valuable feedback on my manuscript but for also helping me become a better writer. I'd also like to thank Eric Koester & the Creator Institute and Brian Bies & New Degree Press for guiding me through the journey of writing and publishing a book.

Thank you so much to everyone who has helped me make my dream of becoming a published author into a reality. Every kind word of encouragement and each piece of advice you shared truly means the world to me.

Last but not least, I'd like to acknowledge you, the reader, for picking up this book and joining me on this journey!

APPENDIX

———

INTRODUCTION

Aguirre, Abby. "Simone Biles on Overcoming Abuse, the Postponed Olympics, and Training During a Pandemic." *Vogue,* July 9, 2020. https://www.vogue.com/article/simone-biles-cover-august-2020.

Billie Jean King Enterprises. "Biography." Firsts and Facts. Accessed November 22, 2020. http://www.billiejeanking.com

Chappell, Bill. "Spurs' Becky Hammon Becomes First Woman to Act as Head Coach of an NBA Team." *Sports* (blog). *NPR,* December 30, 2020. https://www.npr.org/2020/12/31/952295130/spurs-becky-hammon-becomes-first-woman-to-coach-an-nba-team

Driver, David. "Overseas Play a Necessary Part of Life for WNBA players." *Global Sport Matters,* April 16, 2019. https://globalsportmatters.com/business/2019/04/16/overseas-play-a-necessary-part-of-life-for-wnba-players/.

Goal (blog). "USWNT's Olympics Record: How Many Gold Medals Has the U.S. Women's Soccer Team Won?" March 9, 2021. Accessed November 22, 2020. https://www.goal.com/en/news/uswnts-olympics-record-how-many-gold-medals-has-the-us/1hwncb955vs9l1q88ck7byl3vw.

Coyne, Kendall. "About." Kendall's Story. Accessed November 22, 2020. http://www.kendallcoyne.com/about.

Miller, Kerri, and Jeffrey Bissoy. "Women Athletes Deserve More Respect. Why Don't They Get It?" *MPR News,* July 2, 2019. https://www.mprnews.org/story/2019/07/02/miller-women-athletes-deserve-more-respect-why-dont-they-get-it.

Queen Ballers Club (blog). "WNBA Salary 2021: The Lows & Highs." October 4, 2020. Accessed November 22, 2020. https://queenballers.club/basketball/wnba-salary.

SHOWTIME Sports "Alana Nichols: 60 MINUTES SPORTS Full Segment." June 28, 2016. Video, 15:44.
https://www.youtube.com/watch?v=SZHBH7MYLVc&feature=emb_title&ab_channel=SHOWTIMESports.

TuckerCenter. "Media Coverage and Female Athletes - Full Documentary." July 29, 2015. Video, 56:40.
https://www.youtube.com/watch?v=lVqHsMP-GTM&ab_channel=TuckerCenter.

Zimbalist, Andrew. "Female Athletes Are Undervalued, In Both Money and Media Terms." Forbes, April 10, 2019.
https://www.forbes.com/sites/andrewzimbalist/2019/04/10/female-athletes-are-undervalued-in-both-money-and-media-terms/?sh=5c2ad46213ed.

STRUGGLES BEFORE TITLE IX

Girls S.T.E.A.M. Institute. "About Us." We Pioneer Helping Pioneers. Accessed January 16, 2021.
https://girlsteaminstitute.org/.

Rawlings, Matt. "Revisiting the Scots First State Champs," The Outlook, July 6, 2017.
https://pamplinmedia.com/go/45-sports/365420-245917-revisiting-the-scots-first-state-champs.

Women's Sports Foundation. "Title IX and the Rise of Female Athletes in America." September 2, 2016.
https://www.womenssportsfoundation.org/education/title-ix-and-the-rise-of-female-athletes-in-america/#:~:text=Before%20Title%20IX%2C%20one%20in,that%20we%20are%20making%20headway.

THIRTY-SEVEN WORDS CHANGE HISTORY

Barajas, Joshua. "Equal Pay for Equal Play. What the Sport of Tennis Got Right." PBS, April 12, 2016.
https://www.pbs.org/newshour/economy/equal-pay-for-equal-play-what-the-sport-of-tennis-got-right.

Billie Jean King Enterprises. "Biography." Firsts and Facts. Accessed November 22, 2020.
http://www.billiejeanking.com

Billie Jean King Leadership Initiative. "Home." Let's Ignite a Conversation about Leadership and Living. Accessed June 29, 2021.
https://bjkli.org/.

Burk, Martha. "Title IX at 40 — An Interview With Billie Jean King." HuffPost, June 20, 2012.
https://www.huffpost.com/entry/billie-jean-king-title-ix_b_1609164.

Chapin, Angelina. "Four Decades After the Battle of the Sexes, the Fight for Equality Goes On." The Guardian, March 11, 2017.
https://www.theguardian.com/sport/2017/mar/11/billie-jean-king-battle-of-the-sexes-tennis.

King, Billie Jean. "Looking Back, Looking Forward: 40 Years Of Title IX." *HuffPost*, June 23, 2011.
https://www.huffpost.com/entry/looking-back-looking-forw_b_882828.

NCAA. "Title IX Frequently Asked Questions." What is Title IX? Accessed June 23, 2011.
https://www.ncaa.org/about/resources/inclusion/title-ix-frequently-asked-questions.

USA Patriotism. "Presidential Medal of Freedom 2009 Ceremony - Presented by President Barack Obama." October 19, 2011. Video, 35:23.
https://www.youtube.com/watch?v=mb3Pl5000EE&ab_channel=USAPatriotism%21.

GENDER PAY GAP IN SPORTS

Berkman, Seth. "Hefty Raises, Olympic Gold, and Then Crumbs for U.S. Women's Hockey." *New York Times*, April 3, 2019.
https://www.nytimes.com/2019/04/03/sports/us-womens-national-team-hockey.html.

Berkman, Seth. "U.S. Women's Hockey Team Plans to Boycott World Championship Over Pay Dispute." *New York Times*, March 15, 2017.
https://www.nytimes.com/2017/03/15/sports/hockey/team-usa-women-boycott-world-championships.html.

Berkman, Seth. "U.S. Women's Team Strikes a Deal With U.S.A. Hockey." *New York Times*, March 28, 2017.
https://www.nytimes.com/2017/03/28/sports/hockey/usa-hockey-uswnt-boycott.html.

Delmore, Erin. "'We Didn't Back Down': How Women's Basketball Players Scored Major Wins For Equal Pay." *NBC News*, February 6, 2020.
https://www.nbcnews.com/know-your-value/feature/we-didn-t-back-down-how-women-s-basketball-players-ncna1131561

ESPN. "Alex Morgan, Megan Rapinoe Vow to Push Forward After USWNT Legal Setback." May 4, 2020.
https://www.espn.com/soccer/united-states-usaw/story/4091797/alex-morgan-megan-rapinoe-vow-to-push-forward-after-uswnt-legal-setback.

ESPN. "USWNT Lawsuit Versus U.S. Soccer Explained: Defining the Pay Gaps, What's at Stake for Both Sides." June 3, 2020.
https://www.espn.com/soccer/united-states-usaw/story/4071258/uswnt-lawsuit-versus-us-soccer-explained-defining-the-pay-gapswhats-at-stake-for-both-sides.

Ithaca College. "Ellen Staurowsky." Accessed January 28, 2021.
https://www.ithaca.edu/faculty/staurows#:~:text=Ellen%20J.,and%20the%20AAHPERD%20Research%20Consortium.

Pound, Jesse. "Gender Pay Gap for US Soccer Player is 'Untenable Position,' Top Sports Agent Casey Wasserman Says." *CNBC*, July 11, 2019.
https://www.cnbc.com/2019/07/11/pay-gap-for-us-soccer-players-is-untenable-position-wasserman-says.html.

Price, Joe. "These are the Highest-Paid Athletes in the World According to 'Forbes'."
Complex (blog). May 29, 2020.
https://www.complex.com/sports/2020/05/highest-paid-athletes-in-world-2020-
forbes-list.

NEGLECT OF WOMEN'S SPORTS

Azzi, Alex. "All of the Disparities at the 2021 NCAA Women's Basketball
Tournament." *On Her Turf* (blog). March 25, 2021.
https://onherturf.nbcsports.com/2021/03/25/ncaa-womens-mens-basketball-weight-
rooms-discrepancies/.

Stewart, Breanna. (breannastewart). "Sounds About Right, Coming From a Page
That Has Posted Nothing About the Women's Tournament. How Can We Get
Others to Respect Us When The NCAA Doesn't?" Twitter, March 27, 2019.
https://twitter.com/breannastewart/status/1110816500053655552?lang=en.

Durham, Meghan. "Record-Setting 2019 Tournament Concludes with Thrilling
Women's Final Four in Tampa." NCAA. April 23, 2019.
http://www.ncaa.org/about/resources/media-center/news/record-setting-2019-
tournament-concludes-thrilling-women-s-final-four-tampa.

Negley, Cassandra. "Breanna Stewart Calls Out NCAA For Lack of Respect During
Women's Game During March Madness." *Yahoo Entertainment!* (blog). March 27, 2019.
https://www.yahoo.com/entertainment/breanna-stewart-calls-out-ncaa-for-lack-of-
respect-to-the-womens-game-during-march-madness-150554669.html.

PennState Donald P. Bellisario College of Communications. "Marie Hardin."
Accessed January 6, 2021.
https://www.bellisario.psu.edu/people/individual/marie-hardin.

Zimbalist, Andrew. "Female Athletes Are Undervalued, In Both Money and Media
Terms." *Forbes,* April 10, 2019.
https://www.forbes.com/sites/andrewzimbalist/2019/04/10/female-athletes-are-
undervalued-in-both-money-and-media-terms/?sh=5c2ad46213ed.

ALANA NICHOLS

International Paralympic Committee . "Paralympic Sports." List of Sports and
Events. June 25, 2021.
https://www.paralympic.org/sports

Miller, Monica. "4 Female C-Suite Executives Who Played College Sports." NCAA.
March 8, 2018.
https://www.ncaa.org/student-athletes/former-student-athlete/4-female-c-suite-
executives-who-played-college-sports

Presagia Sports (blog). "Let's Talk About Adaptive Sports!" June 4, 2018. Accessed
June 25, 2021.
https://learn.presagiasports.com/blog/lets-talk-about-adaptive-sports

SHOWTIME Sports "Alana Nichols | 60 MINUTES SPORTS Full Segment." June 28, 2016. Video, 15:44. https://www.youtube.com/watch?v=SZHBH7MYLVc&feature=emb_title&ab_channel=SHOWTIMESports.

Women's Sports Foundation. (womenssportsfoundation). "As 2020 comes to a close, we'd like to thank outgoing WSF President @alanathejane for all of the incredible work she's done! With Alana at the helm, our..." Instagram, video, December 31, 2020. https://www.instagram.com/p/CJeUK4QgUaO/?utm_source=ig_web_copy_link

BIGGER THAN THE GAME

Maloney, Jack. "Minnesota Lynx Star Maya Moore to Sit Out 2021 WNBA season to Rest, Continue Fight for Social Justice." *CBS*, March 10, 2021. https://www.cbssports.com/wnba/news/minnesota-lynx-star-maya-moore-to-sit-out-2021-wnba-season-to-rest-continue-fight-for-social-justice/

Moore, Maya. "About Maya." Accessed February 3, 2021. https://mayamoore.com/about/

Montgomery, Renee. "About." Accessed February 3, 2021. https://www.reneemontgomery.net/about/

Renee Montgomery Foundation. "Home." Accessed February 3, 2021. https://reneemontgomeryfoundation.org/

Win With Justice. "About." Accessed February 3, 2021. https://winwithjustice.org/

WNBA. "WNBA Approves Sale of Atlanta Dream to Larry Gottesdiener." WNBA press release, February 26, 2021. WNBA. website. https://dream.wnba.com/news/wnba-approves-sale-of-atlanta-dream-to-larry-gottesdiener/, accessed February 3, 2021.

KRISTI YAMAGUCHI

"1992 US Olympic Skating Team." *The Christian Science Monitor*, January 17, 1992. https://www.csmonitor.com/1992/0117/17102.html.

Active & Safe. "Figure Skating." Accessed December 6, 2020. https://www.activesafe.ca/figure-skating/

Always Dream. "Program." Our Program. Accessed December 6, 2020. https://www.alwaysdream.org/.

Keegan, Kayla. "Kristi Yamaguchi Looks Back on the 1992 Olympics 26 Years Later." *Good Housekeeping*, February 10, 2018. https://www.goodhousekeeping.com/life/entertainment/news/a47856/kristi-yamaguchi-1992-olympics/.

Tong, Traci. "Kristi Yamaguchi Inspires a Record Number of Asian American Skaters." *The World*, February 12, 2018. https://www.pri.org/stories/2018-02-12/kristi-yamaguchi-inspires-record-number-asian-american-skaters#:~:text=Contrast%20that%20to%201992%20at,in%20the%20figure%20skating%20event.

MELISSA STOCKWELL

International Paralympic Committee. "Paralympics History." Accessed December 24, 2020. https://www.paralympic.org/ipc/history.

Triathlon Inspires. "Melissa Stockwell." Accessed June 15, 2021. https://www.triathloninspires.com/melissa-stockwell/.

LINDSEY VONN

Encyclopaedia Britannica Online. Academic ed. s.v. "Lindsey Vonn." Accessed December 27, 2020, https://www.britannica.com/biography/Lindsey-Vonn

Hodgetts, Rob. "Lindsey Vonn Cries over Memory of Late Grandfather." *CNN*, February 9, 2018. https://www.cnn.com/2018/02/09/sport/lindsey-vonn-winter-olympics-tears-grandfather-pyeongchang-intl/index.html.

Vonn, Lindsey. (lindseyvonn). "It's Been an Emotional 2 weeks Making the Hardest Decision of My Life, but I Have Accepted That I Cannot Continue Ski Racing. I Will Compete at the World..." Instagram, photo, February 1, 2019. https://www.instagram.com/p/BtWBLQsnKXD/?utm_source=ig_embed&ig_rid=e7274256-462b-40b9-ac28-e45052aef3d9

McManus, Jane. "'Fearless:' How Lindsey Vonn's Career Is the Dream Actualized." *New York Daily News,* February 10, 2019. https://www.nydailynews.com/sports/more-sports/ny-sports-lindsey-vonn-mcmanus-20190210-story.html.

Meyers, Louis. "Opinion: The Mountains Will Remember Lindsey Vonn." *The Washington Post*, February 15, 2019. https://www.washingtonpost.com/opinions/the-mountains-will-remember-lindsey-vonn/2019/02/15/3d733578-2efb-11e9-8781-763619f12cb4_story.html.

Red Bull. "About Lindsey Vonn." Accessed December 27, 2020. http://www.lindseyvonn.com/.

The Lindsey Vonn Foundation. "About." Accessed December 27, 2020. https://www.lindseyvonnfoundation.org/.

TODAY. "Olympian Lindsey Vonn Talks Retirement, Boyfriend and Birthday | TODAY." February 21, 2019. Video, 7:22. https://www.youtube.com/watch?v=ovI3sq4QyTo&t=215s.

KENDALL COYNE SCHOFIELD
Adidas. "She Breaks Barriers: Kendall Coyne Schofield." March 16, 2019. Video, 1:45. https://www.youtube.com/watch?v=R_0vD36s1ZA&feature=emb_title&ab_channel=adidas.

Benjamin, Amalie. "Coyne Schofield Shines in Fastest Skater at All-Star Skills." NHL. January 25, 2019. https://www.nhl.com/news/kendall-coyne-schofield-shines-in-fastest-skater-at-all-star-skills/c-304238704.

Chicago Blackhawks. "As Fast as Her: Chicago Blackhawks." January 22, 2020. Video, 18:37. https://www.youtube.com/watch?v=5it22DYmjJQ&ab_channel=ChicagoBlackhawks.

Coyne, Kendall. "About." Accessed November 22, 2020. http://www.kendallcoyne.com/about.

Myers, Tracey. "Coyne Schofield Hired as Blackhawks' First Female Development Coach." NHL. November 23, 2020. https://www.nhl.com/news/blackhawks-hire-kendall-coyne-schofield-as-player-development-coach/c-319692898.

USA Hockey. "Girls and Women's Hockey." Accessed November 22, 2020. https://www.usahockey.com/girlshockey.

LAUREN FISHER
CrossFit Games. "Growing Up Strong: Lauren Fisher." September 14, 2020. Video, 8:02. https://www.youtube.com/watch?v=WjVRLpMVHxM.

CrossFit LLC. "About the Games." Accessed November 22, 2020. https://games.crossfit.com/about-the-games.

Grown Strong. "About Grown Strong." Accessed November 22, 2020. https://grownstrong.com/pages/about-grown-strong.

Fisher, Lauren. "About." Accessed November 22, 2020. https://lauren-fisher.com/pages/about.

Quinn, Elizabeth. "How to Cope with a Sports Injury." Very Well Fit. Last modified March 17, 2020. https://www.verywellfit.com/the-emotional-stress-of-a-sports-injury-3120689.

Tzeng, Jolin. "Why Every Woman Needs to Build Self-Confidence." *Thrive Global*, October 15, 2018. https://thriveglobal.com/stories/why-every-woman-need-to-build-self-confidence/.

REVOLUTIONIZING WOMEN'S SOCCER
Bay Area Women's Sports Initiative (BAWSI). "BAWSI." Accessed February 27, 2021. https://bawsi.org/

FIFA. "The 19ers Look to Morgan After Five Star Performance." June 12, 2019.
https://www.fifa.com/womensworldcup/news/the-19ers-look-to-morgan-after-five-star-performance#lindsey-horan-of-the-usa-celebrates-with-teammates-after-scoring

Timm-Garcia, Jaide. "Women's World Cup: The Match That Changed Women's Football." CNN, July 23, 2019.
https://www.cnn.com/2019/05/31/football/usa-1999-womens-world-cup-victory-brandi-chastain-mia-hamm-wwc-spt-intl/index.html

HILARY KNIGHT

Associated Press. "Hilary Knight: Pushing Boundaries." ESPN. ESPN Enterprises, Inc., October 3, 2014.
https://www.espn.com/los-angeles/nhl/story/_/id/11636028/hilary-knight-two-us-olympian-skates-practice-anaheim-ducks

"Hilary Knight." Team USA. Accessed March 3, 2021.
https://www.teamusa.org/usa-hockey/athletes/hilary-knight#profile

Howard, Johnette. "The Shrewd Steps that Led the U.S. Women to Landmark Deal." ESPN. ESPN Enterprises, Inc., March 30, 2017.
https://www.espn.com/olympics/hockey/story/_/id/19042414/us-women-hockey-team-shrewd-steps-led-us-women-landmark-deal

"Professional Women's Hockey Players Association." PWHPA. Accessed March 3, 2021.
https://pwhpa.com/

Rosen, Haley. "The Face of a Movement: Hilary Knight Talks PWHPA, What Comes Next, and What Hockey Needs." Just Women's Sports, April 15, 2020.
https://justwomenssports.com/the-face-of-a-movement-hilary-knight-talks-pwhpa-what-comes-next-and-what-hockey-needs/

Rosen, Karen. "Golden Goal! Team USA Wins First Women's Ice Hockey Olympic Gold Medal in 20 Years." Team USA. United States Olympic and Paralympic Committee, February 22, 2018.
https://www.teamusa.org/News/2018/February/22/Golden-Goal-Team-USA-Wins-First-Womens-Ice-Hockey-Olympic-Gold-Medal-In-20-Years

FEMALE COACHES IN PROFESSIONAL SPORTS

Alfred Verhoeven. "Microsoft - Be The One (2020) Super Bowl with Katie Sowers." February 3, 2020. Video, 1:00.
https://www.youtube.com/watch?v=JhHcI4xPR_k&ab_channel=AlfredVerhoeven

Becky Hammon. "Biography." Accessed February 19, 2021.
https://beckyhammon25.com/index.php/biography/

Brady, James. "How Katie Sowers Became the First Woman and Openly Gay Coach in Super Bowl History." SB Nation (blog).
https://www.sbnation.com/nfl/2020/1/28/21074672/katie-sowers-49ers-first-woman-openly-gay-nfl-coach-super-bowl-history

BSN Sports (blog). "Why Women Coaches Matter" November 16, 2020. Accessed February 19, 2021. https://blog.bsnsports.com/bsn-story/women-coaches-matter

Chappell, Bill. "Spurs' Becky Hammon Becomes First Woman to Act as Head Coach of an NBA Team." *Sports* (blog). *NPR*, December 30, 2020. https://www.npr.org/2020/12/31/952295130/spurs-becky-hammon-becomes-first-woman-to-coach-an-nba-team

Haigh, Mim. "Why Women Coaches Matter." *Athlete Assessments* (blog). Accessed February 19, 2021. https://www.athleteassessments.com/why-women-coaches-matter/

Malady, Matthew J.X. "Sidelined: Why Are There Still No Women Coaching Men's Sports? And Why Don't We Care?" *Slate* (blog). September 28, 2012. https://slate.com/human-interest/2012/09/female-coaches-why-arent-there-more-women-in-charge-of-mens-teams.html

University of Minnesota. "Nicole LaVoi." Accessed February 19, 2021. https://www.cehd.umn.edu/kin/people/nmlavoi/

Zarrett, Nicole, Cheryl Cooky, Philip Veliz. *Coaching Through a Gender Lens: Maximizing Girls' Play and Potential.* New York: Women's Sports Foundation, 2019

WOMEN IN SPORTS MEDIA

LaChina Robinson. "About LaChina." Accessed March 3, 2021. http://lachinarobinson.com/#about

McGough, Michael. "Mary Jo Kane Announces Retirement, Following Decades of Research on Girls and Women in Sports." The Minnesota Daily. September 27, 2019. https://mndaily.com/224224/news/adkane/

Rising Media Stars. "About." Accessed March 3, 2021. https://www.risingmediastars.org/about

FAN ENGAGEMENT IN WOMEN'S SPORTS

DiTrolio, Megan; "How Cathy Engelbert and the WNBA Pulled Off a Slam-Dunk Season."; *Marie Claire* (blog); October 30, 2020; https://www.marieclaire.com/career-advice/a34520502/cathy-engelbert-wnba/.

FIFA. "FIFA Women's World Cup 2019 Watched By More Than 1 Billion." October 18, 2019. https://www.fifa.com/womensworldcup/news/fifa-women-s-world-cup-2019tm-watched-by-more-than-1-billion.

NWSL. "About the NWSL." Accessed January 13, 2021. https://www.nwslsoccer.com/about-the-nwsl.

Team USA. "Pyeongchang Games Recap Part 1: Fan Engagement Through Social, Digital and Broadcast Platforms Reach New Heights During 2018 Games." March 21, 2018. https://www.teamusa.org/media/news/usopc/Fan-engagement-reach-new-heights-during-2018-Games-032118.

The Nielsen Company (US), LLC. "Global Interest in Women's Sports is on the Rise." October 3, 2018. https://www.nielsen.com/us/en/insights/article/2018/global-interest-in-womens-sports-is-on-the rise/#:~:text=A%20survey%20across%20eight%20key,engage%20a%20gender%2Dbalanced%20audience.

WORKING TOGETHER TO ADVANCE WOMEN'S SPORTS

Anderson, Joel. "Steph Curry's Latest Sneaker, Co-designed by 9-year-old Riley Morrison, Releases on International Women's Day." March 7, 2019. https://www.espn.com/espnw/culture/story/_/id/26178047/steph-curry-latest-sneaker-co-designed-9-year-old-riley-morrison-releases-international-women-day.

Buxeda, Camille. "Nine-Year-Old Riley Morrison Writes Letter to Steph Curry." November 30, 2018. https://www.wnba.com/news/nine-year-old-riley-morrison-writes-letter-to-steph-curry/.

Curry, Stephen. "This Is Personal." The Players' Tribune. August 26, 2018. https://www.theplayerstribune.com/articles/stephen-curry-womens-equality.

Low, Asher. "Stephen Curry's NBA All-Star Selections through the Years." March 6, 2021. https://warriorswire.usatoday.com/gallery/stephen-currys-nba-all-star-selections-through-the-years/.

NBA. "It's Our Game - Warriors Basketball Camp." August 16, 2018. https://www.nba.com/warriors/its-our-game-warriors-basketball-camp.

NBA. "Scenes from Curry's "It's Our Game" Camp." August 15, 2019. https://www.nba.com/warriors/news/scenes-from-currys-its-our-game-camp-20190815.

Reid, Storm. (@stormreid). "God Please Help Me to Keep Dreaming of Ways to Make a Positive Impact on Young Girls. I'm Super Excited to Soon Launch an Initiative That I Pray Will Make a..." Instagram, photo. September 1, 2018. https://www.instagram.com/p/BnMsLVohvcP/?utm_source=ig_embed&ig_rid=aof2ffod-b148-42de-956c-e8ff92c763dd.

Rodriguez, Tristi. "Steph Curry Teams up with Chase to Empower Girls, Women with 'Opportunity of a Lifetime'." October 11, 2019. https://www.kron4.com/news/bay-area/steph-curry-teams-up-with-chase-to-empower-girls-women-with-opportunity-of-a-lifetime/.

Curry, Stephen. (@stephencurry30). "When It Comes to Empowering Girls, Oakland High School Is Getting It Done. I Partnered with @chase to Launch the "It's Our Game" Ticket Platform. Every Game..." Instagram, video. October 11, 2019. https://www.instagram.com/p/B3frAETlxgk/?utm_source=ig_embed&ig_rid=51c3b137-917f-4454-808e-3096983bfa68.

Under Armour, Inc. "Inspiring Young Girls to Be Amazing." March 5, 2020. https://about.underarmour.com/news/2020/02/international-womens-day-2020-and-curry-7-bamazing-colorway.

KEEPING GIRLS IN THE GAME

Jr. NBA. "Her Time to Play." Sports Play a Valuable Role in the Development of Young Girls and the Advancement of Women as Leaders in Society. Accessed February 10, 2021. https://jr.nba.com/hertimetoplay/

VIS Holdings Inc. "Voice in Sport." Accessed February 10, 2021. https://www.voiceinsport.com

Women's Sports Foundation. "Home." Accessed February 10, 2021 https://www.womenssportsfoundation.org/

Women's Sports Foundation. "Do You Know the Factors Influencing Girls' Participation in Sports?" Accessed February 10, 2021. https://www.womenssportsfoundation.org/do-you-know-the-factors-influencing-girls-participation-in-sports/

Zarrett, Nicole, Philip Veliz, and Don Sabo. *Teen Sport in America: Why Participation Matters.* East Meadow: Women's Sports Foundation, 2018. https://www.womenssportsfoundation.org/wp-content/uploads/2018/01/teen-sport-in-america-full-report-web.pdf

YOUNG GIRLS MAKING CHANGE

Gordon, Samantha, and Ari Bruening. *Sweet Feet: Samantha Gordon's Winning Season.* United States of America: Walker Children, 2013.

UTGFL; "Tackle Football League for Girls Growing Fast in Utah"; *Utah Girls Tackle Football (blog)*; October 28, 2019; https://www.utahgirlstacklefootball.com/post/tackle-football-league-for-girls-growing-fast-in-utah.

Valkyrie Football. "NFL Honors Utah Girls Tackle Football with Game Changer Award." June 21, 2018. Video, 6:59. https://www.youtube.com/watch?v=7W_qyjFUor4&ab_channel=ValkyrieFootball.

Williams, Serena. "'We Must Continue to Dream Big': An Open Letter from Serena Williams." *The Guardian*, November 29, 2016. https://www.theguardian.com/lifeandstyle/2016/nov/29/dream-big-open-letter-serena-williams-porter-magazine-incredible-women-of-2016-issue-women-athletes.